Kindness is Courageous

100 Stories to Remind You People Are Brave and Kind

By Nicole J Phillips

D1370016

Table of Contents

Introduction

Have you ever looked at our world and seen darkness? Yeah, me too.

Actually, we don't even need to look around. We can sit in one spot with our eyes closed wearing earmuffs and still feel violated by the rush of bad news pounding the airwaves.

Violence, drug epidemics, human trafficking. The negativity is clawing it's way to the top of our consciousness, blocking the view of the good.

Negativity likes to pretend it's the only show in town. It's like a Vegas marquee, obnoxiously bright and loud and impossible not to notice.

So we see it, but just like we don't stand on the sidewalk staring at signs, we have to be careful not to give negativity too much attention.

The idea isn't new. There is a beautiful Native American legend of two wolves. A man at one of my speaking events shared it with me. It goes like this:

> An old Cherokee is teaching his grandson about life. "A fight is going on inside me," he said to the boy.
>
> "It is a terrible fight and it is between two wolves. One is evil – he is anger, envy, sorrow, regret, greed, arrogance, self-pity, guilt, resentment, inferiority, lies, false pride, superiority, and ego."

He continued, "The other is good – he is joy, peace, love, hope, serenity, humility, kindness, benevolence, empathy, generosity, truth, compassion, and faith. The same fight is going on inside you – and inside every other person, too."

The grandson thought about it for a minute and then asked his grandfather, "Which wolf will win?"

The old Cherokee simply replied, "The one you feed."[1]

The acts of kindness in this book are meant to feed the good in your life. They are meant to remind you that people are brave and kind, that *you* are brave and kind.

Most of the stories originally appeared in *The Forum of Fargo-Moorhead* and the company's affiliated newspapers in North Dakota and Minnesota.

The Forum has graciously allowed me to write a weekly column, "Kindness is Contagious," since 2011.

People from across the country (and one guy in Canada) send in their anecdotes of kindness - something they've done and how it made them feel, or how kindness showed up for them at just the right moment, and I run them in the newspaper.

I have the happiest email inbox on the planet.

By the way, if you have a kindness adventure you'd like to share, please send it to me at info@nicolejphillips.com.

---

[1] http://www.virtuesforlife.com/two-wolves/

Back in 2016, I took 100 of readers' favorite stories and published my first book, *Kindness is Contagious: 100 Stories to Remind You God is Good and So Are Most People.*

My hope was that people would begin to notice the kindness in their own lives when they increased their awareness through a daily story instead of a weekly one.

Feedback from that book has blessed my socks off. People say it's inspiring them to do an act of kindness each day, give people the benefit of the doubt, and forgive quickly. There is even a family in Brazil who is learning English by reading through my book together. How cool is that?

Here we are with 100 more stories in *Kindness is Courageous.* When I think of that title, I think again of the words brave and kind.

Brave and kind are the two words that have always shaped my life: as the flower girl in my mom's prison chapel wedding when I was ten, to competing in the Miss America pageant when I was 22, to being diagnosed with breast cancer on my 40th birthday.

Many times in my life I've needed to borrow other people's bravery. I often still do. My goal with this book is to also be able to extend it to others.

You might not think you have it in you to talk to a weathered-looking woman without a home, to ask about her story, to remind her she's not invisible, but you do.

When you do, the life you transform won't be hers. It'll be yours. The more intentional we are about kindness, the more it changes us.

Researchers have found, regardless of our age, we are constantly forming new pathways in the brain. It happens every day based on the situations we encounter and how we react to them. React with anger and that becomes your brain's go-to mechanism. React with compassion and your brain begins to look for the good and veer toward positivity as a first response.

So yes, there is bad in the world and it's obnoxiously loud. Don't let the noise pollution fool you. The world is full of people who are brave and kind. Their kindness is contagious and courageous, and so is yours.

Your acts of kindness will change the world, because they will change you. And I'd say a brave, kind you is just what the world needs right now.

Boy Serves Kindness with a Side of Chicken

When my son started bringing home information about his sixth grade graduation, I thought it was cute. There would be a ceremony and a class party and even some donated prizes.

Then I found out some of the parents were giving their children gifts to celebrate the milestone.

I am all for using any excuse possible to celebrate life with ice cream, but in our house, gifts are reserved for birthdays and major life events.

Sure, the kids are moving from the elementary school to the middle school, but as we gently explained to our son and his sister (who was graduating from eighth grade), we expect you to make it all the way through high school. Once that's done, we'll talk about gifts.

Luckily for another sweet boy I know, other families have other traditions.

Marcus, a fellow sixth grade graduate, was given $25 by a family friend for the occasion.

Now, I should pause and tell you that Marcus doesn't have a lot of excess in his life. He's never known his father, his mother is in prison and his grandma does what she can each day to keep the family afloat.

In this kid's eyes, a $25 cash gift is a windfall.

Marcus did what all kids in our town do when they find themselves suddenly wealthy: he took his loot to Walmart.

As his grandma pulled into the parking lot, Marcus noticed a family sitting on the curb with a sign indicating they were homeless.

Marcus carried on and headed into Walmart on a mission to find something spectacular, but as he looked at aisle after aisle of games and toys, he couldn't get that family out of his mind.

Eventually he gave up and headed over to the deli counter. That's where he found a warm, pre-cooked chicken dinner.

With only his little brother in tow, Marcus bravely took the chicken to the cash register, paid for it with his graduation money, and then walked out of the store.

He headed straight for the homeless family and quietly handed them their next meal.

The exchange was brief and nearly silent. Marcus isn't much for words, but I'm certain his actions spoke quite loudly to everyone who witnessed the series of events.

After that, Marcus got back into his grandmother's car and asked her to stop at Wendy's so he could buy his little brother a Frosty. Ice cream seemed to be an appropriate way to top off such a special afternoon.

When I asked Marcus about that day, he didn't have a lot to say. He said he just saw a need and knew that he could fill it, so he did.

I asked him why he bought the family food instead of giving them cash. I could see the wisdom of a boy who has seen much of the darker side of life.

"I wanted to make sure they didn't spend the money on bad decisions," he said.

Ah. I let those words settle in my mind and in my heart.

Despite knowing the hurts and needs and temptations of this world, in one brave and kind move, Marcus proved that kindness is a powerful antidote.

There Is a Marcus in Your Life

A letter came to my house the other day, but it wasn't addressed to me. It was for a 12-year-old boy named Marcus.

No return address and stamped at a post office two states away. Hmmm.

"Hey, Marcus, you got some mail!" I yelled from my office.

"Me? Who's it from?" he asked as he ambled into the room.

"No idea. Open it."

As he peeled open the envelope and silently read the card, I got to witness all of the emotions of the world in his face. Curiosity, trepidation, and confusion turned into joy, pride and awe.

"Will you read it to me?" I asked as he stood there silently.

I could tell he was choked up and wasn't surprised when he shook his head and said, "No. You read it."

By the time I finished reading the anonymous letter, I was choked up too. Here is what it said.

"Dear Marcus, Ms. Nicole Phillips has written many stories about kindness, but my favorite was reading about you and the chicken you gave to the homeless family.

You are going to do big things with your life, Marcus.

I believe in you and know God has great plans. Hope you will use this gift to buy some ice cream."

Inside that envelope was a crisp $50 bill.

The generous donor was referring to a column I had written a few weeks before called, "Boy serves kindness with a side of chicken."

Marcus lives with his grandma. His mom is in prison and he doesn't know his dad.

He had been given $25 from a family friend in honor of his sixth-grade graduation. Instead of spending that money on himself, Marcus bought a chicken dinner for a homeless family.

What nobody, including the anonymous donor, could have known was that the day after Marcus bought that dinner, his house burned down. Literally. To the ground. A few of his baseball trophies and photos were fine, and no one was hurt, but the house is gone.

Marcus is living with us while his grandma finds a new home.

The person who sent me the letter obviously knew I would know how to find Marcus. That person just didn't know Marcus would be sitting on the couch in my living room.

I got a front-row seat to see what happens when someone breathes encouragement into a young person's life. Let me tell you, it's spectacular.

Marcus was stunned by the money, but he was immeasurably touched by the words.

Those four sentences told Marcus that someone saw him. That his attempts to bring good into the world matter. That his challenging circumstances don't define or defeat him, but instead build character and values.

Let me tell you a secret: There is a Marcus in your life. There is someone, young or old, who needs to know you see them. They are on a rough path and they need to hear words of affirmation.

You have those words to freely give. Please don't hold them back.

Dog and Boy Form Special Bond Thanks to Trainer's Kindness

Danette Jensen lives in Goodridge, Minnesota, about 70 miles from the Canadian border. She and her husband run DJ's K9 Country, a boarding facility with more than 20 kennels and a large training room.

I guess you could say Danette is dog crazy. She is certainly an expert in the field. She has a radio show and people call in with their canine quandaries.

But perhaps more than caring for the dogs and training them, Danette loves the unique way she gets to help others through her calling. She shared with me one of the many stories she has about pairing a pup up with the perfect family.

"I have trained dogs since I was 8 years old, starting at the 4-H level and working my way up to becoming a professional dog trainer and behaviorist.

I train service dogs to help with numerous types of situations, including those who are wheelchair bound or suffer from PTSD, seizures, diabetes, emotional disorders and autism to name a few.

I grew up with a brother with special needs who had frequent grand mal seizures. He would often hide, and my mother would tear around the house saying, 'Can't you train a dog to find him?' So now, search and rescue is a large part of the autism training I do.

I received a call from a woman who sounded tired, like she was running out of options. This is not the first or last parent to contact me in this emotional state.

The mother has four children with post-traumatic stress disorder, and she was hoping to find a service dog.

I blurted out that I had two dogs that might work for such an occasion and agreed to meet the family.

The son, who was to be paired with the dog, smiled from ear to ear and reacted with such excitement that he brought his mother to tears. She hadn't seen him get excited or smile like that since the traumatic incident years earlier.

I drove away, praying I hadn't opened my mouth and given false hope to the boy, only to see him get disappointed again. I could not handle doing that to this poor child.

Two days later, the family made the three hour drive to spend the day getting to know my dog. I repeatedly said there were no guarantees that this would be the dog for him, but I hoped God was at work!

The meeting went amazingly well, so well that I even let him take the dog that day.

That night, the dog got very anxious and was running around his room. Come to find out, the boy needed to go to the hospital for compacted bowels, which is common for PTSD sufferers.

From that time forward the boy and his dog have become quite the team.

We have now paired the brother with his own dog, and they are going through the bonding portion of their training."

Danette tells me that the first brother and his dog have passed the Public Access test and they are now a certified team, created by kindness.

Many People Benefit When We Strive to Become Our Best

I have yet to meet someone who says, "Nope. I'm not a kind person and I have no intention of changing."

We might agree that we have a little work to be done in the kindness area, but generally people seem to think they are doing a pretty good job of treating others well.

In a study of 100 young people with gang affiliations, the kids rated their level of kindness as "high" and cited evidence such as, "I help my mom carry in the groceries."[2]

It's rare when we can both see our deficiencies and are also willing to do the hard work of changing ourselves for the better.

Sometimes it's easier to go through life on autopilot, but as Lori from Ohio shares, when we really strive to become our best selves, we alter the way others do life as well.

"In my Bible study, we recently decided to do a weekly act of kindness, and then share our adventures with the group when we meet.

That in itself has been quite rewarding.

I have also been listening to The Kindness Podcast and have been encouraged and motivated to start my own personal kindness challenge, aside from my Bible study 'homework.'

---

[2] Barbara Hirsh, http://www.livekinder.com

During this time I have been talking through my experiences with my husband, Tim, not realizing how contagious kindness really is.

One night, Tim came home from the gym holding his sweaty clothes in his hands. With a quirky grin on his face, he asked me, 'Would you like to know why I am carrying my clothes?'

He went on to explain that he had been changing in the locker room after his workout and right across from him was a man who appeared to be homeless getting ready to shower.

My husband noticed that the bag the man was using was very worn and actually had a large hole in the side.

When Tim asked him about the bag, the man told him in a shocked and defensive tone that he has had this bag for years and uses it to carry his food.

Tim said, 'I noticed the hole' and without hesitation, my husband emptied his athletic bag and gave it to the man.

The man was a little taken aback but graciously accepted it.

When Tim came home and shared that story I was elated and very proud of him. He said 'I did my act of kindness for the day' but then hesitated, waiting for my reaction.

What shocked and maybe even disturbed me was how surprised my husband was by my response. He said he thought I would be mad since I had given him that bag.

Wow, was that a self revelation! I couldn't have started my kindness challenge soon enough. I guess kindness really is contagious."

Not only has Lori been changed by her efforts to be more kind, but so has her husband, and now even a stranger at the gym is benefitting.

Blanket Project Ties High School Friends Together

They say there are ties that bind, things that happen in our lives that leave us forever connected and intertwined with others.

But what happens when decades begin to deteriorate our communication with those people?

As Caryl Kiser from southeastern Ohio shares, those ties not only continue to hold, they grow stronger with each knot of kindness.

"Five years ago, after moving back to Ohio from Chicago, I met a classmate, Sonja, for the first time in about 50 years. We were in the car chatting when she said she wanted to stop and buy some fleece material. She was hoping to learn how to make a tie blanket. Well, I knew how and offered to help her make one.

A few days later, Sonja and I learned that our former classmate had been diagnosed with breast cancer. We quickly agreed we would make her a blanket. Another classmate was also diagnosed with breast cancer, so we made a second blanket.

Sonja and I contacted a few other classmates to help tie the knots on the blankets and offer prayers of healing for our friends.

As we made the blankets, we caught up on life after years

apart. We chatted about ourselves, high school and the ups and downs since our teenage days.

We soon learned that another classmate had lost his life to cancer. We made a third blanket to give to his wife, who, yes, was yet another classmate!

It was then that we officially decided to make blankets for those who needed healing prayers. Once word was out about us and our project, the Gallia (Ohio) Academy High School, Class of 1967, sent us donations for our blanket project. We became known as the 'Blanket Ladies' and continue to be supported by the men and women of the Class of '67.

To date, we have made more than 600 blankets which have been sent throughout the United States. We donate most of our blankets to the cancer center in our original hometown of Gallipolis, Ohio. Our youngest recipient was six months old.

This little core group of 10 women have been in Girl Scouts and church camps together. We have giggled over boys, held each other through breakups with our boyfriends, wiped away tears of disappointment and walked across the stage on graduation night before stepping into life.

Most of us were only in touch periodically until five years ago when the Blanket Ladies group formed.

During that time, our group has once again held each other in love through two diagnoses of breast cancer, one heart attack, one life-threatening emergency surgery and six funerals for parents, siblings and children.

We are more than classmates. We are sisters who have a bond that will never be broken!"

I wonder if all those years ago, Caryl and her friends learned the "Make New Friends" Girl Scout song. They certainly are living out the lyrics. *Make new friends, but keep the old. One is silver, the other is gold. A circle is round, it has no end. That's how long, I will be your friend.*

A Single Act of Kindness Spans States and Decades

Our lives often intersect for a reason, but isn't it amazing when they do, and we actually notice?

Two men, one from Twin Valley, Minnesota, and the other from Loveland, Colorado, have never met in person, but their paths crossed 20 years ago, leading to a beautiful act of kindness today.

Here is their story:

"In October 1998, I was traveling to Colorado for an elk hunt. Each member of our group brought along a significant amount of cash to pay for food, horse rental, licenses, etc.

During our one-night stay at the Best Western in Loveland, Colo., I lost the checkbook where I had hidden my 12 $100 bills. I asked at the desk if it had been turned in, but no one had seen it.

We continued on with our trip, with me borrowing from my fellow travelers. The thought of losing that amount of cash weighed on my mind, but I just had to try to enjoy the beautiful scenery of Colorado and learn a lesson from the experience. After receiving no contact from the hotel, I was resigned I would never get the money back.

A few weeks later, on Thanksgiving weekend, the supervisor from the Best Western in Colorado called us at 7 a.m.. An employee during the night shift had decided to go through the lost and found and discovered my checkbook and its contents.

The supervisor mailed it to me, and sure enough, it was all there.

I ended up sending a reward to the employee, named Roy, who found the checkbook, and I also sent a letter to the corporate office. Not long afterwards I received a Christmas card and thank you letter from Roy in which he said this:

I am at one time, ashamed at the thoughts that occurred to me when I discovered your wallet, and proud to have made the right decision to return it to you. At an earlier time in my life, I would probably not have been so honest. I plan to use this reward to treat my wife to dinner and make a holiday gift of pet food to the humane society.

In March of 2018, after going through old stuff, I came across my hunting maps from Colorado and the Christmas card from Roy. It's now nearly two decades later, but I decided to contact him and see if I could send him an additional reward just for fun.

I found him, thanks to Google, and proceeded to tell him my name and how our lives had intersected nearly 20 years ago. It all came back to him, and we had a pleasant conversation. Much to my surprise, Roy told me he still works at the Best Western. I asked for his current address so I could forward another reward to say thank you again.

After receiving the gift, Roy called to thank me. He said his wife is scheduled for surgery in April and because of the gift, they are able to have a ramp built for easier access to their home."

Even across many years and many miles, a quick interaction between two strangers continues to draw kindness.

Lean Into the Storm to Show Kindness

I was standing in the shower sobbing. With the fan on and the water running, it was the only place in the house I could hide until my torrent of pain had been released.

Never before had I needed to expel so many emotional toxins from my system. And never have I needed to again. But back in May of 2015, I was walking through a breast cancer diagnosis, and I was scared.

The rest of my family was scared, too. I had already picked out my husband's future wife. You know that creepy game you play where you tell your spouse that, if you die, they should marry so-and-so? Wait. Am I the only one who's ever played that game?

Anyway, Saul was as terrified as I was and he did not appreciate the way I was planning my demise, even if it was for his benefit.

We both tried to be strong and confident for the kids, but there were days when the doubt creeped in and started wrapping its bony fingers around our brains.

I was having one of those days. That's why I was standing in the shower sobbing when Saul walked into the room.

He was alarmed at first. "Baby, are you okay?"

"Go away! Just let me cry." I know I should have been more gentle with my rejection of his concern, but I could only deal with one person at a time. At that particular moment, I was dealing with me.

I thought he would mumble a hurt or embarrassed, "OK" and walk out of the room, but that's not what he did. Instead, he leaned in. Fully dressed, he literally leaned into the shower and figuratively leaned into my pain.

We were both sopping wet by the time he reached over and shut off the faucet, then pulled a towel around me. We stood there in the shower for a few minutes, him just holding me, letting me get it all out.

How often do we want to help someone, but are afraid of their reaction? We hurt for them and long to extend kindness, but we are hesitant because we don't want to add to their burden or create an even bigger mess.

My husband's bold foray into the shower that day sticks with me because of the valuable lesson it taught me: it's important to step into someone else's storm.

That person who is hurting so badly might not want to walk over to you and get too close because they are protecting you from getting wet, from feeling the full encumbrance of their grief. They seem standoffish, while in reality, they would love a friend.

We often feel like grief is contagious and we don't want to spread it around, so we keep it to ourselves. But in my experience, what's revealed is what's healed. When we sit with someone, even in the silence because there are no words to say, we are bringing light and love to the battlefield.

May I remind you today, as I remind myself, that grief is not contagious. But kindness sure is.

Kindness has
the power to
permeate
prison walls.

Kindness Reaches Through the Thickest of Walls

I went to visit a friend in prison a few weeks ago. It was the first time I had been in the belly of a correctional facility since I was a child. Back then, I went with my mom to visit her husband. This time, I got to escort a young friend to see his mom.

Two different prisons, one for men and one for women, decades between those experiences, and yet my eyes saw the same thing now that they did when I was a kid: people who just plain look like people.

Sure, we could tell which ones were the inmates because they all wore matching uniforms, but beyond that, they just looked like regular, everyday people.

I think perhaps I expected to see something in their eyes that made them different from me, more evil somehow. Maybe it would be something in the way they held themselves. But no. What I saw were people smiling, laughing, weeping a little and beyond grateful to be able to love on their friends and family who came to visit them, who had not locked them out even though they were locked in.

An inmate from the James River Correctional Center in Jamestown, North Dakota sent me this letter about the kindness he is seeing inside the prison walls.

"I read your column when I get the chance, and it makes me think that there are truly good and compassionate people in the world. Anyway, I am writing to let you know that even being in prison, you can find kindness.

For example, the newborn baby girl who was found alive after her mother was murdered in Fargo, I believe her name is Haisley Jo.

Well, a lot of us here behind bars felt for her and her family, and we all started a collection for her. The Warden was so taken aback at our willingness to help that he allowed us to take money from our R.A. (Release Account) to donate.

Now we don't make much here, it's anywhere from $1.15 to $5 a day. Some people have to pay fines and child support out of that, and then the R.A. takes 25 percent of what's left.

Anyway, what I'm trying to say is, we don't have a lot, but what we have, we are willing to give.

Funny how some of the nicest people you'll ever meet are rough looking and covered in tattoos.

Keep your columns going. They are reaching through even the thickest of walls."

You never know where you'll find kindness, which is why it's so important to always be on the lookout for it. When you find it, you'll be blessed. Kindness has the power to heal lifelong hurts, crack through age-old biases and even permeate prison walls.

Listen to Your Gut for Kindness

People often ask me for ideas about doing random acts of kindness. They want something that doesn't cost a lot or is perhaps free. Something that will be impactful, but not too time consuming. Something that the whole family can be involved in or an act that will create a bond with a difficult coworker.

A quick Google search shows no fewer than 16,000,000 results for "ideas for random acts of kindness."

Ideas are out there. We have created the wheel over and over and over again. So instead of telling people what to do, I tell people to slow down and listen.

Ever heard of a gut instinct? It's that feeling deep inside our bodies that says, "Do this" or "Don't do that."

When we listen to our gut, we stay out of trouble, but we also open up a huge avenue for kindness.

Life becomes incredibly fun when we go about our daily activities looking for someone in our path who could use a little pick-me-up.

Anything we do to love on another person matters. We can go wild with creativity or simply say "Yes" to that voice inside that nudges us to do a quick act of service.

As Dorothy from Minnesota shares, kindness comes in lots of different forms, and they are all greatly appreciated.

"I am a widow in my 80s who would like to share an act of kindness with you and your readers.

A family, who are friends of mine, are always doing kind things for me. The father helps with anything around the house that needs doing. The older children, who are teenagers, have shoveled my driveway and sidewalk. I have a pear tree and apple tree, and they come over and help pick up the fallen fruit.

Getting back to my original story, last year, I had foot surgery on the ninth of March. I was unable to go to the St Patrick's Day parade so they decided to have a parade for me.

They brought over a bag with hats, necklaces and even a bowtie for our dog. They told me to get decorated, and they would be coming by with a parade. They put two chairs out in my driveway, one for me to sit in and one to prop my healing foot.

First came the youngest girl doing cartwheels down the sidewalk, even though the temperature was about 30. Next came the son, dressed up and leading their boxer dog with his bowtie. Next came the mother, leading their other boxer dog also dressed up, followed by their other daughter who was pulling a wagon decorated like a float.

After they were all past they came back and gave me hugs and boxes of candy, for both me and my dog!

I was overwhelmed and blessed that they thought to do this for me."

Souper Bowl Puts Kind Spin on Big Game

Super Bowl Sunday: the best time of year to buy a big-screen TV or football-themed paper plates. The hype behind the biggest game of the year has become its own beast.

In 2017, the cost of one of those 30 second commercials we all love to watch will go for $7.7 million. Yikes.

Back in 1990, a seminary intern at a church in South Carolina said a little prayer: "Lord, even as we enjoy the Super Bowl football game, help us be mindful of those who are without a bowl of soup to eat."

That prayer gave birth to an idea that has spread and multiplied many times over. For nearly three decades, youth-led groups across the nation have been using Super Bowl Sunday as an opportunity to collect money and canned goods for local food banks. It's called the Souper Bowl of Caring.

If you ever wonder if a few people and some spare change can make a big impact, here's just one example.

Our Savior's Lutheran Church in Moorhead, Minnesota has been participating in the Souper Bowl project since 2003.

Last year, through the efforts of six kids, they were able to donate $284 to the Dorothy Day Food Pantry. The year before, four kids collected $164 and 10 food items.

Even more impressive is the cumulative effect of those years of service. In the past 14 years, the youth in that church have donated $3.5K and 263 items.

The Souper Bowl of Caring group explains the benefits for both the individual communities and the volunteers.

"...ordinary young people have generated more than $100 million for soup kitchens, food banks and other charities in communities across the country. In addition, hundreds of thousands of youth have experienced for themselves the joy and satisfaction of giving and serving, inspiring people of all ages to follow their generous example."

Sometimes we overthink things or make them big and complicated, at least I do. To me, that's the beauty of the Souper Bowl. It's as work-intensive or relaxed as the kids want to make it.

For example, at Our Savior's, the note in the newsletter asks people to bring a canned or boxed item along with any loose change to the church services on Super Bowl Sunday. That's it.

The power comes from the thousands of youth groups across the country doing the exact same thing on the exact same day. Since each group gets to give their donations to the local charity of their choice, we end up with a nation of soup bowls being filled for the hungry.

Yes, the game is fun and so is the hype, but adding a little kindness to the equation creates a winning game plan every time.

You can get involved with the Souper Bowl of Caring project or learn how to start your own group at **souperbowl.org.**

Kindness Saves Grandmas From Speeding Ticket

I've mentioned before that my husband affectionately calls me Gordon Leadfoot when I drive. It's his humorous (to him) way of combining one of his favorite musicians with my tendency to always be in a hurry.

Several speeding tickets to my name, I've gotten much better at obeying the law, but there are still times when I feel like my absolute need to be somewhere creates a valid reason to speed. I know. I'm sorry to all the law enforcement officers reading this. I'm wrong. I'm working on creating better habits.

Anyway, I had to giggle when I got this story from Sarah Tachon in Evansville, Wisconsin. A fellow mom and kindness advocate, she found herself rushing for a good reason. She didn't get caught, but she was mortified by who did.

"A group of us enjoy cooking and decided to prepare a meal before the winter break to bring to the kindergarten through second grade teachers' lounge for lunch.

We were excited for the challenge of feeding 50 to 60 hard-working teachers. They like Asian food, so I asked my 'authentic' Chinese friend, Maggie, to lead the group.

There were about six of us gathered for grilling and chopping at my house. Many of these people are playgroup friends and are home during the day, but our little group also included two grandmas who volunteered to help. We assembled an awesome meal of stir fried noodles, potstickers and an Asian slaw salad and loaded it into the car.

Maggie and I hopped into one car and 'the grandmas' followed in another to help set up at the school.

We had eight minutes to get there before the second grade teachers would be arriving for lunch.

Racing down the highway, my heart sank as I went right past a police officer waiting to catch speeders. 'This could ruin everything,' I thought to myself 'and all because of a bad choice to speed.'

Luckily, the officer didn't pull out to follow me, but when I looked back, I could see his flashers go on behind the grandmas' car. Oh no! This is even worse! They were just trying to help and now I've gotten them pulled over because I was speeding and they were following.

I whipped my car around, pulled up behind them and begged the officer to let them go. I told him we were bringing food to the school and had only six minutes left to get there. We offered him some noodles from the car, but he politely declined.

The officer let the grandmas go with a verbal warning and a smile. We were trying to show kindness to the teachers, but ended up having kindness given to us."

I bet the next time Sarah's group assembles to cook up some kindness, they'll be delivering it to the local police station.

"I know true gifts are the gifts of people, and no store or online shopping site could ever match the gift of kindness."

Gratitude Paves the Way for Healing

It's humbling to realize that while I was sitting on the living room floor watching my kids tear into the colorful assortment of presents under the Christmas tree, other lives were unfolding simultaneously in ways much different than mine.

Jayne Holtgrewe of Moorhead, Minnesota spent her day nursing her husband back to health after he experienced a terrible fall.

But instead of grieving for what has happened or what may be to come, Jayne's heart is full of gratitude. She knows that the right people in the right place at the right time saved her husband's life.

She is certain that kindness was the greatest gift she received this holiday season, and she wants to be sure to say thank you to all involved.

"As I sit in this hospital room with my husband, waiting and watching for every sign of healing, I think about how I wouldn't be here had it not been for some wonderful neighbors and good Samaritans, who saw a problem and stopped to help.

With all the ice and slippery roads we have been dealing with here in Moorhead/Fargo, my husband took a severe fall on our driveway a couple days ago.

Unfortunately, I was not home, but for some reason my neighbor came home for lunch that day, not a typical routine for her. She saw him slip and fall backwards on the concrete and immediately took action.

By chance, two more angels just happened to be driving by and stopped to help a stranger. Between the three of them, they were able to help him into the house and then proceeded to call the police, fire department and an ambulance.

Without their quick actions, my husband could have laid there for who knows how long. Time is of the essence when someone has a head injury, and because of the kindness of strangers, an incredible neighbor and our fantastic community's heroes in uniform, I am able to sit here, in this hospital room, with my husband.

How do you ever thank anyone for that gift?

If that were not enough, yet another angel arrived from across the street and shoveled and scraped down my driveway and front steps. I'm sure he thought nothing of his act of kindness, but after I spent a very long day at the hospital, his gift was exactly what I needed.

My husband, I'm happy to say, is showing signs of healing, small steps, but steps nonetheless in the right direction. I'm hopeful each day he will improve and get stronger.

I know true gifts are the gifts of people, and no store or online shopping site could ever match the gift of kindness."

May we all walk into the New Year realizing each and every day, without fail, all we have been given and all that we have to give.

A Christmas Kindness Story

It's our stories that build the color into our lives. Yes, there is often pain as they are being written, but without that pain we wouldn't know real joy.

I want to spend this week and next sharing the story of a mom and her teenage son, and the beauty that unfolded when one act of kindness led to the next.

"My son was a freshman in high school. I was a single mom. Money was always tight. It was December and I had less than $20 to fill the gas tank, put food on the table and keep money in my son's school lunch account until payday.

I was struggling with how best to stretch my dollar when my son bounced in the door and announced he needed a ride to HuHot Grill and $10 for dinner for his school's DECA meeting. Gah! $10 was almost all the money I had! As I looked into his innocent face, I didn't have the heart to say no.

There wasn't much to eat in the house, so I went through the couch cushions and coin purse to see if I could muster up enough to get a $.99 burger at Wendy's when I dropped him off at the party.

We headed to HuHot, him excited, me feeling the sinking desperation of a black hole I never seemed to get out of. I pulled in front of the restaurant and waved goodbye before heading to the drive-thru for my burger.

It was December in North Dakota, and it was bitterly cold. I pulled up and gave my order to the unappreciative voice coming out of the speaker.

I pulled forward to the window to pay and painstakingly counted out each coin, praying I didn't drop any on the floor.

Feeling frustrated with my slowness while he sat with his drive-up window open, the young man growled at me to 'Hurry up' because it's cold. As I handed over my coins, I apologized but quipped back at him that perhaps it would be better if he wore his coat when he worked the drive-thru window in winter.

The young worker surprised me when he said he wished he could. He said he didn't have one after his dog chewed his to shreds. He had to walk a good distance to work, but was hopeful that in a few weeks he'd have enough money saved up to buy a coat.

Ugh — me and my smart aleck mouth. I looked at his face and thought of how alone in the world he must be, if no one was around to help him buy a coat, in winter, in North Dakota.

Here I wanted him to have sympathy on me and my struggle, but the truth was, we both had struggles of our own.

I began to slowly pull away from the window, when my phone rang. I put down my burger and answered the call.

My friend's husband, a pastor, asked if I was home because he had something he wanted to drop off that couldn't be left outside.

I raced home to find this dear man standing in my entryway with a big box. 'Every year our church does food baskets for a holiday meal. I thought of you and your son,' he explained.

Then he handed me two envelopes. 'One is a gift card to the grocery store, and here's an extra gift.'

Inside the second envelope was a very generous gift card to Walmart. I tried unsuccessfully to hold back the tears as I thanked my friend.

I picked up my son from his Christmas party and began to regale the events of the night to him as he listened in amazement. Then I looked at him and said 'Nathaniel, I think we need to go to Walmart and buy a coat.'

'I was thinking the same thing, Mom.'

We examined every coat in the men's section for style, warmth and durability. After our very concentrated efforts, we selected a coat and then swung through the gift wrap section for a big bag and some tissue paper.

I pulled up to the Wendy's drive-thru for the second time that night feeling almost giddy. But what was I going to say? I hadn't thought this part through. Then that voice came over the tiny menu speaker: 'Can I take your order?'

'Well no. I was here a little earlier. Can I pull up to the window?'

When the window opened I thrust the bag at a very bewildered looking young man.

'What's this? Who is this for? Who is this from?'

'It's for you. Merry Christmas. I want you to know that God loves you and this is a gift from us to you.'

'But you don't even know me.'

'Doesn't matter. I know you needed a coat. Stay warm and have a good night.'

I waved and pulled away from the window. Awkward, but amazing! Really amazing.

As we slowly drove away, Nathaniel watched as the young man tried the coat on in front of his co-workers. They were smiling and admiring the jacket. A few were even crying.

We drove home on a cloud that is hard to describe. My son spoke the words I was feeling. 'Mom, I feel so good right now. I've never felt so good before!'

Yep, I thought, me too. No money could ever buy that feeling of blessing someone who really needs it."

It's the backdrop of pain in our lives that gives our joy such brilliance. And often, it's receiving an act of kindness at just the right time that spurs us to do the same for others.

Kids Will Remember Kindness in the Classroom

I packed a bag lunch for my second grader this morning. Actually, he packed it for himself, but I stood guard making sure there was something other than sugar in his noontime meal. The last thing that kid needs right now is sugar. Ben is pumped so full of end-of-the-year adrenaline that I say a little prayer for his teacher each day as I usher my 8-year-old out the door.

Field trips, final chapters during story time, throwing away old crayons and crumpled papers... there is something special about the end of the school year.

I know teachers often send their students off to summer break wondering if the late hours and lesson plans even made a difference. I've had friends question aloud if what they've taught will stick.

You know what I tell them? The kids will remember your kindness.

They may forget that "i comes before e except after c", but they will remember the warm smiles and the encouraging words.

I was walking through my son's school a few weeks ago when I noticed hand-drawn pictures of kindness pasted on the walls. And not just one wall.

Everywhere I went in the school I saw small signs that read, "Kindness makes smiles," "More kindness, more smiles," and "Be kind today."

Each one was signed by The Kindness Ninjas.

I wondered which classroom was responsible until I stopped in to say hi to my third grade teacher friend, Liz.

Ms. Liz was sitting in a rocking chair with her class gathered around her feet. She looked at them conspiratorially and whispered, "Should we tell Mrs. Phillips about our secret?" The class voted to let me in on their weekly mission to spread kindness throughout the school.

They went on to tell me about writing chalk messages on the playground, secretly putting notes in library books and sending digital cards to a student in the hospital. Then they fessed up about the Kindness Ninja signs.

They talked about sending a smile around the room and seeing how many smiles they could "collect" from others during the day.

Those are the lessons that will stick. I know because I could see it in their faces. They got it. They understood the power of kindness and how to use it to reroute a bad day.

I'd say to Ms. Liz, and all the other teachers out there who make kindness a priority in the classroom, mission accomplished. Well done. Your kindness matters.

Now pull out the sunscreen and go enjoy your summer.

No Need to Plan Kindness this Season

Are you done? Have you finished all the hustle and bustle that comes with creating the magic of the season? If so, good for you! (Now can you come to my house and help me?)

If not, take heart. Ironically, it's in the midst of our craziest schedules that we are most blessed with the chance to show other people they are not alone.

Maybe you adopt a family for Christmas or pull a child's name off a giving tree. Maybe you donate canned goods to the food bank or serve a meal at the homeless shelter.

Please don't feel discouraged if you haven't planned any specific charitable acts. The most beautiful opportunities for kindness will come to us if we go about our business with one eye on our own needs and one on the needs of others.

A woman named Mindy was shopping with her daughter in Janesville, Wisconsin, when they came across someone who looked like he could use a little holiday magic.

"We were checking out at Walmart and there was a man behind us who looked like he didn't have a lot of money. We actually thought perhaps he was homeless. He was waiting to buy a box of candy when my 14-year-old daughter, Mia, whispered in my ear, 'Mom, you should pay for that guy's stuff.' I thought that was a great suggestion, so I added his candy to our bill, and we headed out of the store.

As we were walking to the van, I said, 'You know I should have given him the $20 bill that was in my wallet, too." My daughter agreed.

While unloading our groceries I said, 'If I give it to you, will you walk back to the front of the store (where he was sitting outside eating his candy) and give it to him?'

Mia got really nervous and said she didn't know if she could. I tried to calm her nerves by reminding her how cool it would be and also said, 'If it makes you feel any better, you'll probably never see him again, so you don't need to be embarrassed.' She decided she would go, despite her nerves.

She bravely walked back to where the man was still sitting and said, 'Hi, sir, my mom and I wanted you to have this.' I was so proud of her.

The man thanked Mia in a somewhat timid voice.

After the exchange, I asked my daughter how she felt. As we talked about how maybe that box of candy was his only meal for the day, and how good it feels to help, she wondered aloud why we feel so nervous reaching out to others. I'm not sure, but I think we all have that hesitation of embarrassing the other person."

Kindness certainly carries a risk, but the reward we get as the giver is more precious than anything we could find in a stocking or under a tree.

Stop Wondering - Your Kindness Does Matter

Does what I do matter?

Have you ever thought that to yourself?

Perhaps you've been in the checkout lane when the cashier asks if you'd like to donate a dollar to end world hunger. Or maybe you've dropped off old towels and blankets so they could be sent to some area of devastation overseas. Most recently, I was asked to donate bottles of water to the hurricane victims.

Does the little bit we do for others make a difference? It's hard to know when the solution is slow coming and we never actually see the people benefitting.

How or why we're helping can get a little hazy.

Willard Hiebert of Moorhead, Minnesota had the amazing opportunity to hear directly from someone who had been the recipient of others' goodwill. It happened more than 50 years ago, but Willard still remembers it today.

"In the spring of 1964, I was an exchange student at the J.G. University in Mainz, Germany.

One evening I went to hear a speech by the U.S. ambassador to Germany in the largest room at the university. The room was packed.

The ambassador gave his speech on the goals of U.S. aid around the world and used the term 'benevolence' in it.

After the speech during a question and answer exchange, a student from an African country stood up and challenged the ambassador saying that what the U.S. was doing wasn't benevolence at all but more or less a bribe for loyalty.

As I recall, before the ambassador could answer, an older German man got up and said the following: 'After the war (WWII) we had little food to eat and very few clothes. We were hungry and cold. Then the care packages started to arrive from America. They were a godsend and I call that benevolence.'

He sat down but the whole audience of German students who had experienced that era first hand rose of one accord and applauded wildly. I was never so proud to be an American!

Almost every time I tell this story the listeners get tears in their eyes. In my opinion, this simply shows that kindness is the best diplomacy."

It wasn't just one person's generosity the man received after the war, but the collective, powerful kindness of a whole country. It made an impact that spanned the decades.

The next time your heart tells you to help, but you're wondering if it even matters, I hope you remember there is someone out there who is grateful that you care.

Let's Turn Black Friday into RAK Friday

In my family, instead of Thanksgiving turkey, we pull out the all-holiday ham. We will continue pulling it out for leftovers for the next week, starting today: RAK Friday.

Oh, I'm sorry. Did you think it was called Black Friday? Nah, that's so 1990s. You know, when people loved standing in line overnight to get the new superfly boombox with detachable speakers? Or pulling a total stranger's hair to get her out of the way when she was reaching for the last Cabbage Patch doll? Okay, maybe that all happened in the '80s, but you get my point.

Thank goodness we've evolved.

The Random Acts of Kindness Foundation explains the theory behind this growing movement on their website.

"Random Acts of Kindness (RAK) Friday is a grassroots effort to create an alternative and kind start to the holiday season.

Since Black Friday is not going away anytime soon, #RAKFriday makes the best out of the situation and uses the captive audience to spread as much kindness as possible.

Science proves that when one person commits a random act of kindness for another, it not only positively affects both the giver and the receiver, but it also impacts the bystander who witnesses the act of kindness.

Think of all the potential bystanders one act of kindness would have during Black Friday shopping. A lot. And lots of bystanders = potential to create a HUGE positive impact."

Imagine buying a $5 gift card to go with the early morning coffee you grab at the drive-thru. You put it in an envelope (the gift card, not the coffee) with a little note wishing the recipient a Happy RAK Friday and inviting them to treat themselves to a treat after their shopping.

Then you find that lady in the toy aisle who is looking forlorn because the last of the Tickle Me Elmos has been cleared from the shelves. You hand her the card with a big smile and go about your day.

Her perspective changes, you feel delighted to brighten someone's outlook, and the 40 people standing nearby feel warm and fuzzy because they witnessed the interaction.

Or maybe you do what my father-in-law does and stock your wallet with band-aids. Then when he sees a child looking in need of a little special attention, he pulls one out. (Usually, it's one of my children who needs the band-aid, but that's another story.)

Or maybe you will commit to opening the door for people and smiling at them.

The feel-good chemicals will be flowing freely, even if the checkout lane traffic isn't.

We can make this happen. We can decide what our holiday season will look like. And we can start today, turning Black Friday into RAK Friday.

Kindness Works as a Trifecta

I have written more than 300 stories for this column, but I'd have many more to share if it weren't for one tiny phrase that keeps repeating itself in a variety of forms.

"I don't want to toot my own horn."

"I hate to brag."

"If I get my rewards on Earth, I won't get them in Heaven."

"I was taught to give in private."

Now I love the humble heart behind this sentiment, but I learned something recently that has changed the way I think about those responses.

I got to talk with Brooke Jones, the Vice President of one of the world's largest kindness organizations, the Random Acts of Kindness Foundation, for my podcast.

We were talking about the four feel-good chemicals that are released into the body when we do an act of kindness for a stranger.

Endorphins relieve pain. Serotonin is the body's natural anti-depressant. Dopamine makes us feel happy and rewarded. Oxytocin, the cuddle hormone, reduces our blood pressure.

That all made sense to me, because I had heard it before. But then she said something remarkable. It's not just the giver or the receiver who gets the chemical benefits of kindness.

She said kindness works as a trifecta. The giver, the receiver and *the witness* all benefit from the release of those hormones.

That means when you're at the grocery store and you pay for the person in front of you who doesn't have quite enough money, you benefit (as the giver), the shopper benefits (as the receiver) and the clerk, bagger and anyone else waiting in line all benefit as the witnesses.

One act of kindness can start a tidal wave of good feelings.

Knowing that you can have these major health benefits by seeing goodness in the world is exciting, and we don't have to wait to stumble upon kindness.

Review the good things you see each day before you shut your eyes for the night.

Fill your social media feeds with positivity by following groups that intentionally post uplifting stories.

Ask people to share their favorite kindness story with you when you meet for lunch or coffee.

Get your kids into the habit of noticing kindness by asking them what they did to be kind that day or what they saw someone else do. This opens up great conversation around the dinner table or as you carpool to and from activities.

The goal is to be intentional about looking for the kindness around you so that it becomes second nature to instantly see it.

My hope is that when we open our eyes to the good that is happening, we will want to contribute to it, both privately and publicly.

Perhaps eventually, you will feel bold enough to share your own stories because you'll know that by reliving them, you aren't being "braggy" or conceited, but are actually helping even more people get those feel-good chemicals flowing.

A Free Lunch Fills a Belly and a Soul

When we talk about feeding the hungry, we usually talk about feeding people who literally don't have enough to eat. There are kids in my area who grab a bag of chips from the convenience store because it's cheaper than buying a sandwich and an apple. It's also cheaper than paying for the school lunch if they don't quite qualify for free meals.

Yes, there is a desperate need to feed people in a physical sense. In a world with so much excess, it's tragic that anyone goes without the basic necessities like food.

But sometimes we also need to provide for people who are hungry in other ways. Maybe you know a woman who is spiritually starving. Or a young man who could use a mentor because he is thirsty for wisdom. Perhaps there is someone who is about to cross your path who just wants connection. They simply want to know that they are seen.

Louise Thomsen from Perham, Minnesota, has a special message she wants to share with a few people she hopes will be reading this column. Her soul was fed recently by strangers when she sat down for a meal with her husband.

"We are an elderly couple. We have been married 67 years. My husband joined the army when he was 17, right after high school graduation. His mother had to sign for him so that he could enlist.

He was in the reserves and served again when the Korean conflict broke out. We were married by then and it was a long, hard year for us — being newlyweds and him so far away. He returned and we lived our lives and had our family.

Three years ago, my husband had a stroke. He limps badly now when he walks, but his attitude is great and we continue to enjoy our lives.

On Friday, Oct. 13, we drove from our home in Perham, Minnesota, to Fargo, North Dakota to attend Grandparents Day at our grandson's school. We stopped in Dilworth at the Perkins restaurant for lunch. We had a wonderful meal.

Imagine our surprise when we expected the check and instead, the cheerful waitress told us that the people in the booth behind us had not only paid our bill, but wanted us to have a piece of pie, too!

Thank you to our unknown benefactors. You made our day and the good feeling you gave us surrounded us like a happy cloud."

It doesn't matter whether someone can afford to pay for their own lunch or not. In a world that is starving for kindness, the question is — can we really afford not to?

Am I teaching my kids to be kind?

Ride Home Opens Door to Life-Changing Kindness

When I think about the very first acts of kindness I can recall, I think about my mom. I remember her teaching English as a Second Language (ESL) in our small town. How scary it must have been for her students to move to a new country and not know how to communicate. My mom felt their apprehension and gave them her language and her heart. In exchange we often had beautiful handmade gifts or delicious treats in our home that spoke of deep cultural roots.

Sarah Tachon, grew up, just like me, watching her mom live out kindness. She still remembers one story in particular.

"My mom's name is Karen, and she is Chinese from Taiwan. She and my dad met in the Peace Corps in the '70s in Malaysia where he was teaching her English. They fell in love and moved to Madison, Wisconsin, where he finished getting his PhD in Water Chemistry.

When I was about 10 years old, my mom took us to an Asian grocery store to buy some food you can only find there. My sisters and I were waiting in the car. The next thing we know, my mom comes back to the car with a tall Asian man. Mom told us his name was Yu. She had just met him in the checkout line and was giving him a ride home.

At the time, this didn't seem too strange.

We were used to mom doing things like this. She was often giving rides, bringing food, visiting people who were house bound and helping families navigate the cultural differences here in America.

We visited Yu in his student apartment, where we also met his wife, who was Chinese and a magician. As a kid, I remember they made us some weird food and she showed us cool tricks. Neither of them spoke much English, so there was a lot of head nodding and smiling.

Yu was a music student at the University of Wisconsin. He had moved here from China with his wife to get a degree and build a better life. Yu and mom stayed in touch even after he and his wife moved to Florida to continue his studies.

One night, Yu called my mom in a panic. His wife was pregnant again and they were certain they couldn't afford a child. They didn't know what to do and were considering aborting the baby. Mom talked Yu and his wife through this scary situation. She told them about God's love and plan for this baby and urged them not to have an abortion. She also connected them with a Pro-Life group in their area.

Yu and his wife listened to my mom and welcomed a baby boy into the world.

Mom just showed me a picture of the beautiful family, and I think the son just graduated from college. It is an amazing story of God's work that started with an act of kindness to smile, say hi and give a stranger a ride home."

Kindness Happens When We Take Time for Others

It's the question that guides most of my parenting decisions: Am I teaching my kids to be kind?

I don't want them to be doormats or people who bend to the will of others even when it's dangerous or unhealthy. But I do hope they find a good balance in life and lead with kindness whenever it's possible.

The truth is, I have to do my best and then hope for the best, because I may never really know. They spend all day in school and evenings in various activities that don't include me. Are they the ones who are shaping the school into a loving, inclusive environment or are they the bullies?

I can take an educated guess, but sometimes it's just nice to know. Knowing often comes because other people are kind enough to tell me about the good they see in my children.

Fellow mom, Angela Marks, got a glimpse into her son's behavior thanks to an attentive librarian and a free pizza. Here's her story:

"One day after football practice, my son, Ryan, was walking past the junior high soccer game happening on a neighboring field. He ran into his high school baseball coach and they stopped to catch up for a bit.

While they were talking, a girl who has some mental challenges was yelling for him to come talk to her in the concession stand. He excused himself from the conversation with his coach to go and talk to the girl.

She was fascinated with his football jersey and wanted to see it and touch it. Ryan was happy to oblige. After several minutes, he left to go change.

It just so happens that the school librarian was also in the concession stand. She was really impressed with the way Ryan handled the situation. In fact, she was so in awe of what he did for the girl, because it made the girl so happy, that she told the vice principal at the high school about his actions.

The vice principal was also moved by Ryan's choice to give a few moments to the girl. He brought him into his office and thanked him for what he had done and gave him a certificate for a free pizza. Ryan was a little confused by all the fuss and told the vice principal that stopping to talk to the girl was just the right thing to do.

The vice principal explained to Ryan that oftentimes, people fail to do the right thing, even when they know they should. In fact, he told Ryan he was so impressed that if he had a million dollars to give away, he'd give it to him, but since he didn't, the free pizza would have to do."

The kindness in this story isn't limited to Ryan. I see it in the coach who stopped to talk with a kid who loves baseball; the girl who made the football player feel noticed; the librarian who passed along what she saw; and the vice principal who took time to reward the good. I also see it in the mom who shared this special story.

Kindness Can Be Found in Life's Details

I got to spend the last week traveling around the state of Wisconsin talking about my favorite thing: kindness.

Unfortunately, going from small town to small town meant I had to do a lot of my least favorite thing: driving.

I was feeling too frugal to spend the extra $5 on cruise control for my rental car, so for eight days, I kept one eye on my lead foot and the other eye on the road.

I was on the second lag of my trip when I started lamenting in my head about my lack of ability to teleport.

This would be so much simpler if I could just snap my fingers and be there.

Normally, when I drive I use it as an opportunity to return phone calls or sing along to my favorite songs.

Not this time. My Ohio-based cellular service was not in the mood to communicate with Wisconsin's rural communities. Neither was the car radio. Just when I'd get a great '80s, '90s or Today station dialed in, static would creep up around the next bend.

Speaking of the next bend, I was never quite sure what was around it because Siri refused to give me driving directions.

So, there I was, fluctuating between 25 and 55 mph on the back roads of my home state, hoping desperately I was going in the right direction.

That's when I saw it: a huge sign nailed to a tree. It simply said, "Smile more."

Then I passed an apple stand, with a small bucket to leave your money. Then came a pumpkin patch with a maze carved out for the littlest trick-or-treaters. Then I noticed a quaint farmstead that someone had worked awfully hard to restore to its original beauty. Then an old school house that probably once doubled as a church.

In each little town, high school kids were laughing and painting the storefront windows for homecoming.

I noticed a change happening in my heart as I drove day after day, past new hidden treasures. I became grateful for the silence, for my lack of cell phone service and radio stations and Siri's impersonal commands.

Had I been able to teleport from place to place, I would have missed so much. I had time to ponder the kindness of the person who carefully hung that "Smile more" sign and the farmer who blazed the corn maze trail, and the one who offered apples on the honor system.

Instead of worrying about North Korea or pondering whether or not people should stand for the National Anthem, I got to see America. I got to see what's happening in the small spaces that are making a big impact on the culture of their communities.

I have to say, I left Wisconsin feeling so good about the state of our world, because despite what may or may not be happening in the large-scale news events, there is still kindness happening in the details of everyday life, reminding us that things aren't so bad after all.

Kindness Has a Way of Circling Back Around

Anytime is a good time for kindness, but receiving it is especially sweet when you feel like you've got nothing left to give.

Proud dad, Scott Wright, who lives near the Wisconsin/Iowa border, and his wife still remember one particular act of kindness that came when they needed it most.

"Rewind in time. It's May 18, 2000. My wife is 27 weeks pregnant with twins and her water breaks in the middle of the night. We rush to the emergency room, where the doctor advises transferring to a hospital in Iowa City as a precaution. The plan was to stay in Iowa City for six weeks and then return to Dubuque to deliver our twins.

I overheard the phone call to the transport nurse at 3AM. 'Take your time and even take a shower. This is a non-emergency.'

It's about a two-hour drive to Iowa City and my wife arrives around 6AM. They take her to a room and a person brings in a mountain of paperwork to start the intake process. My wife says she needs to use the restroom.

The next thing you hear is my wife screaming.

Well, I'm not sure how to explain it any other way than to say, Maggie, my daughter, was born in the toilet.

They cut the cord, wheel my wife off to a delivery room, and 10 minutes later Kylie is born.

My daughters were born at 27 weeks, one weighing 1 pound 12 ounces and the other weighing 2 pounds 6 ounces.

The girls spent the first two years of their lives on oxygen 24/7, not able to leave the house or hospital.

My wife and I were what I would call 'middle class' income folks. She was the payroll manager of a small private college and I had a growing business. My wife quit her job for obvious reasons, and there were many extra expenses living in a hospital 100+ miles from your home, but we were still able to make ends meet.

Many folks reached out to help us monetarily that first year, but one act of kindness really stands out.

Once a month, for almost a year, we received a handwritten envelope addressed to Mr. and Mrs. Wright. Inside the envelope was a $100 bill.

There was never a note attached, but my wife and I strongly believe that this gift was from the mom of a good friend of ours. We had done repeated favors for her over the years and refused to allow her to pay us.

Now fast forward 17 years. My girls are successful seniors in high school. They are on the honor roll and involved in every sporting activity and social event a high school student would ever want.

They also have a job — babysitting the grandsons of the person who gave us those $100 bills over 17 years ago.

Nothing has ever been said about the money, but it's amazing how kindness has a way of circling back around."

Can We Trust the World to Be Kind to Our Kids?

I was walking through Walmart the other day watching parents and their college students prepare for a new chapter in their lives. It occurred to me in the middle of the toothpaste aisle that it doesn't matter if your kid is going into kindergarten or college, letting them go is hard.

We have to trust that the world will be good to our babies, and that's a hard thing to believe sometimes.

My childhood friend shared a story about her daughter's school talent show. I'm hoping it will remind you, like it did for me, that we can count on kindness to see our kids through.

"As a kindergartner, my daughter, Pietja, [pronounced Peech-ah] sang 'My Favorite Things' from 'The Sound of Music' in her school's annual talent show. She did great, but was disappointed that another student chose the same song.

For this year's talent show, she wanted ideas for songs that would be unique. It's hard to think of things that are age-appropriate but not blockbuster Disney favorites. I suggested Dolly Parton, among other things. She gave Dolly a listen and somehow decided that '9 to 5' really spoke to her as a first-grader making her way in the cut-throat world of a suburban Milwaukee (WI) elementary school.

Pietja had her tryout, and the music teacher loved it and suggested that she use a blonde wig that the school had from last year's play. (Thankfully nobody suggested my daughter try to emulate Dolly's other famous assets.)

Pietja decided yes, that would be great. She also wanted to wear a business suit like an office working woman. My daughter was all in.

I felt like this was all fun and spunky — until right before the show, when I began to worry that maybe this skit was a bit out there. Maybe it wouldn't be relatable, and just kind of weird, to most of the elementary school kids who would not have heard the song before.

I didn't want anyone making fun of her or crushing her spirit. Please remember, she was not wearing this stuff to be ironic. This was 100 percent sincere. She was feeling like the most sophisticated office girl, high heels and all.

I was nervous. But I shouldn't have been. Not only did the kids in the crowd start clapping along and cheering like crazy for her, but when she got off the stage she got high-fives and hugs when she re-joined her classmates on the gym floor.

And it was't just her — the kids gave the same supportive treatment to the boy trying to stack solo cups into a pyramid, the brother and sister pair attempting stand-up comedy, and the little Irish dancer who had a cast on her arm and fell down, but got back up. It was awesome. It looked to me like they recognized the bravery before them and commended it sincerely."

Hearing my friend's story helps me believe that the world and it's people contain enough kindness to see our kids through. I hope it helps you believe, too.

Kindness Makes Kid MVP of the Game

When I first married my husband, he bought me a book called "Basketball for Dummies." He was an assistant men's college basketball coach at the time. I was more interested in the team's colors and cute apparel than in what was happening on the court. We clearly had some work to do.

I asked him to buy me the book for Christmas. I read it cover to cover. I still don't know beans about basketball.

I figured that would be the only sport that I'd really have to pay attention to. I could fake interest at an occasional Super Bowl party.

Then came my boys.

My 11-year-old son, Charlie, has played center on his football team for the past 2 years. Since he was always in the middle of the field holding the ball, he was pretty easy to spot. This year, he came home and excitedly announced he would be moving positions. Something about receiving and catching and running and trying not to get tackled.

You guys, my brain can't contain or retain sports information. I am trying. Truly. It just hurts.

I tell you this because I'm hoping you'll give me grace when I share with you this touching kindness story that happened at a recent sporting event.

On a beautiful July evening, a throng of University of North Dakota fans flocked to Minneapolis for UND night at Target Field. The Twins were taking on the Orioles.

A family friend from Fargo, North Dakota made the four hour road-trip so his boys could see a professional baseball game. One son is in sixth grade and the other is a freshman in high school. Both are big-time baseball fans. They were hanging out in the left-field stands watching batting practice when our friend excused himself to go to the bathroom. Wouldn't you know it, that's when the excitement happened?

Apparently, the outfielder caught a ball that came flying out toward the stands. He then turned around and threw it into the crowd, right to my friend's older son. This was a big deal. The left-field bleachers were filled with hundreds of kids (and a number of adults) hoping to catch a ball during batting practice.

That ball would have looked awesome on my friend's mantel. They probably could have gotten one of those cute, clear little boxes to keep it in. It would have been a special souvenir from a father-son outing.

It might be on a shelf somewhere, but it's not on my friend's shelf. That sweet, sometimes shy, often quiet 14-year-old boy caught the ball and then turned around and gave it to the little kid who was standing next to him. Not his brother. A complete stranger.

When asked why he did it, in a totally endearing teenage boy fashion he said something along the lines of "we have enough baseballs already," and sort of shrugged.

The Twins went on to win that game. They beat the Orioles 9-6. There were even fireworks after the game. It's too bad there isn't a highlight reel for kindness, because that kid's thoughtful action would have totally made him MVP of the game.

A Tree Full of Kindness

My dad had a stroke in the summer of 2016. For more than a year, he's been a resident of an assisted living home. It's a lovely place, but my heart hurts because I know that isn't where he wants to be.

I returned to Wisconsin to visit him a few weeks ago and was delighted to see that he can now do a pretty good shuffle-walk. He still can't move the right side of his body, but he's learning how to compensate. His hard work is paying off. There were tears in both of our eyes when he told me that he gets to move back home this fall.

All the while we were sitting and talking, my boys were enthralled with my dad's window, specifically the view outside my dad's window.

Knowing that my father is a huge bird watcher, some family members installed a perch and a few feeders. My uncle keeps them stocked with seed and my dad has constant feathered friends.

It's a little thing, but it speaks great love to my dad. It turns out, that sort of kindness may not be unique to my father's situation.

A woman from Duluth, Minnesota sent me this touching letter.

"One of my friends lives in a complex for senior citizens. One of her neighbors is confined to a chair and obviously does not get out very often, especially not on his own. His name is Ted, and most times Ted sits by his window and either sleeps or stares at the tree outside.

Other residents in the building have sort of adopted him, and they take turns making sure the tree is decorated. On all occasions, the tree is decked out with appropriate decor: flags and banners for the Fourth of July, lights and colorful decorations for the Christmas season, and flowers and pinwheels with delicate white lights for the summer.

Also, when people enter or leave the building, most of them will stop by the window and wave to Ted, or show him what they've brought, just to make sure he has a smile for the day.

I think these same people are responsible for the flowers and plants in front of his window.

I had to take a picture when I passed by. Stuff like this just gets to me every single time I see it.

There are a lot of horrible things out there, but there are also a lot of plain, ordinary everyday people who do what they can to brighten up the world. These are my heroes."

In the midst of pain or sadness, these heroes quietly fill our lives with joy by their unsung acts of kindness. May we know them. May we be them.

Kindness is a Matter of the Heart

A few weeks ago, I posed a question about the difference between helping others because it's the "right thing to do" or because you want to do an act of kindness. I've already published some answers in this column, but I received one more letter in the mail that I couldn't let go before sharing with you. It's from Jean Lemmon in Fergus Falls, Minnesota.

"Where does citizenship end and kindness begin? The two actions derive their source from two different areas, the head and the heart.

When we were children, our parents taught us a set of rules.They ingrained into our young minds a sense of right and wrong. Hopefully, they demonstrated those rules by their own actions.

But we all reach adulthood and begin making our own choices based on what foundation was given to us. We keep some past rules and others we toss by the wayside.

In reaching that age of 'accountability,' we start thinking for ourselves. We often realize there is something far deeper than us that rules the 'soul' of our lives. When we make contact with the creator of our soul, the heart decision-maker kicks in.

The citizenship decision-maker acts on messages he was told were good deeds. The heart decision-maker is motivated by love from the creator, not parental love or a society role model.

Remember the story of Pinocchio, the little wooden boy whom Geppetto loved so very much?

His nose kept growing longer and longer for every lie he told. When he was sitting in the belly of the whale, he had a transformation. Our little wooden boy became real because of his creator's love.

Good citizenship derives its source from good role models. Kindness derives its source from the soul maker."

I think Jean does an excellent job of pointing out the difference between citizenship and kindness. Between the lines, I also see her providing inspiration to those weary of doing good. Perhaps we need to ask ourselves, Am I doing this because society tells me I have to or because I feel so loved that I just have to pour it out onto others?

Go Fly a Kite

If someone tells you to "go fly a kite," you can pretty much assume he or she is not leading with kindness and a future get-together is not in the works.

Much like the phrases "bug off" or "take a hike," the origin of "go fly a kite" is a little hazy.

Some people believe it came from the stock market crash of 1929, when little pieces of paper were tossed out the window. Others believe it had something to do with a conversation between Benjamin Franklin and his wife.

Either way, when Harvey Laabs left the chill of North Dakota's winter to head south earlier this year, kites and kindness became synonymous.

"I was fascinated by the tricks the pilots performed at the South Padre Island Kite Festival this past February.

Individuals could make their kites literally dance to the music, while teams played 'follow the leader' in a zig-zag course through the sky.

These were not the kites that we flew as children. These kites had multiple control strings. Talented pilots could steer them in any direction they wished.

My curiosity led me over to the team area for the Austin 'End of the Line' Kite Team. They were a friendly group of six who had formed a team a couple of decades ago.

Jim, one of the members, asked me if I had some spare time.

He led me over to the practice field, bringing one of his kites along. He showed me how to stake out the line and set up the kite in preparation for flight. I watched closely as he pulled and pushed with his hands, directing the kite to fly up, then left, then right, then down and on and on; he made it look easy. After several minutes, he brought the kite down to a soft landing.

Then he did the unthinkable. He handed me the lines to his $300 kite! It didn't take long to find out that what Jim made look easy, wasn't easy at all. I managed to get the kite in the air, but keeping it there was another story. Jim coached and encouraged me for 20 minutes as I made many attempts to keep the kite in the air. My most successful flight lasted almost a minute. Most flights ended in a rather dramatic crash into the ground. Miraculously, the kite survived through all of this.

A few days later, I contacted Jim and thanked him for helping me. I told him of my plans to purchase a kite of my own. Jim replied that he was glad to help.

As I reflect on what Jim did, I realize it was much more than teaching me to fly a kite. He gave me his time and showed great kindness in his willingness to go out of his way to help a stranger."

It sounds like for Harvey and Jim, "go fly a kite" is now a way of saying "Let's spread some kindness through the air."

Mom Uses Kindness to Teach About Differences

Taryn Skees is a mom just like me. She's a writer and a speaker who is passionate about the power of kindness.

But Taryn's drive to spread the message of kindness didn't come from a spontaneous act of kindness that transformed her life. It came from the birth of her son.

Taryn's 9-year-old son, Aiden, has a rare craniofacial condition called Apert syndrome. He is one in 160,000, which Taryn knows makes him awfully special.

But it also means that along with cleaning up Cheerios and teaching her child his ABCs, Taryn has to teach the world to see her son the way she does.

"The first few years were trying and scary. Lots of appointments, therapies and surgeries. Through it all, we dealt with stares, whispering and unkind words about our child's differences. I'm not going to lie, it hurt.

Eventually I decided that if I was going to give Aiden a chance at a normal life then I had to become his advocate. I made small 'awareness cards' that I handed out in certain situations where someone was staring or had questions. It had a link to my blog where they could read about Apert syndrome and ways to talk to their children about differences. Sometimes it broke the ice enough to start a conversation and allow me to turn a potentially hurtful situation into an opportunity to educate.

When Aiden started school, I brought in a little book I had made, 'All About Aiden', and read it to the class. I found that once kids knew it was okay to be curious and ask questions, they began to see Aiden as a kid just like them.

Once Aiden was in elementary school, I approached the school with an idea for a project to help kids of all ages who face any number of challenges from divorce to illness, ADHD to having to wear hearing aids. We called this the 'Choose Kind Library' and filled a small nook of the school's library with a special area where they could find books on all these types of issues.

We decorated it with bright colors, printed special spine labels and provided bean bag chairs for kids to have a comfortable space to read. The message was inspired not only by my son, but by the bestselling children's fiction novel Wonder by RJ Palacio.

I am on a mission to continue to spread kindness in any way that I can. We have found that it is not only impacting Aiden and his confidence, but it is helping kids understand that when it comes to disabilities, a little kindness goes a long way!"

For more information on the kindness Taryn, Aiden and her entire family continues to spread, please visit www.MoreSkeesPlease.com.

A Question of Kindness or Citizenship?

You know what I just realized? I do not know the name of the woman who delivers my mail.

Usually my mail carrier just leaves the letters in the box by the road and eventually I wander out and collect them. But every few months, she pulls her truck into my driveway and hops out to hand me a package or a post-vacation bundle of mail.

I always smile and say thank you, but in the three years that we've lived in this house, I never once thought to ask her name.

I got a letter from a man who used to deliver my mail in Fargo that really got me thinking about just how much I miss when I'm lost in my own little world.

"I delivered mail to your house in north Fargo. I never met you there, but I did see Saul and your little children out and about on the bicycle. He remembered me and would always greet me. Please pass on to him how much I appreciated that.

As a letter carrier of 20 years, I often found myself in situations that called for a helping hand. I've found lost cell phones, returned a lady's purse, given directions, detected a natural gas leak, called 911 during a crisis, found a wandering child, stumbled upon people passed out, and much more.

One icy, cold and snowing day, I found a guy from one of my mail routes wandering down the sidewalk with only one shoe on. The other foot was bare. He kept falling down.

I called the police and then followed him until help arrived. The police thought he was drunk, but I've never seen him like that before. He likely could have been experiencing a medical situation. I don't know, nor do I need to know. It felt good to help, but it more seemed like the right thing to do.

So now I'm wondering, can a person differentiate between doing an act of kindness and doing what one 'should' do? As a good citizen, one is expected to just step in and help. Where does citizenship end and kindness begin?"

Hmm ... good question.

I often talk about stepping out of our comfort zones and experiencing that "Helper's High." But the truth is, we need more kindness in this world whether it comes with an adrenaline rush or not.

Sometimes life puts opportunities in our paths to help someone, and we do it because we feel like we should. I think kindness comes into play during those situations when we give just a little more than is necessary.

Like, instead of just thanking the mail carrier for the package, we take a moment to ask her name. Then we work hard to show her she is valued in the future by actually remembering it.

So is that kindness? Or does kindness require an extra step?

Here are some thoughts from readers sent in when I posed the question, "Where does citizenship end and kindness begin?"

Teresa said she would like to be called a "Kind citizen."

Colette mentioned that kindness gets stifled because we live in a society that insists on suing people when things go wrong. Instead of taking a chance, we keep to ourselves.

Barb said she thinks kindness and citizenship "run right into and through each other."

Patt Jackson from Duluth, Minnesota bravely took on the question with this email:

"A few summers ago, I bought a box of junk at an auction (such fun!) and after taking out the things I thought I'd use, I was on my way to deliver the rest to a thrift store. In the box was a pair of men's slip-on leather shoes that looked barely worn, but I didn't know anyone who could use them.

I was stopped at a red light when an older man crossed the street in front of me, dressed shabbily and completely bare-footed. I pulled over and dug the shoes out of the box and offered them to him. They seemed to be a perfect fit.

I was happy and he seemed happy. Was it serendipity?

It made me start thinking about how simple it is to help someone, or brighten someone's day, even just by saying hello.

Now that I am retired, I have made it my mission to do something nice for a person at least once every day, whether it is in person or over the phone or by mail. (I'm a firm believer in handwritten 'thank you' notes.) It takes so little time and effort, and I always hope it will spur someone else on to do the same. Plus, it gives me that 'helper's high' that you mentioned. Not a bad feeling!

Your question about citizenship and kindness is a tough one for me to answer. They seem very similar to me. Years ago a friend made a comment that stuck in my brain, and I try to live by it, though of course I sometimes fail. She wisely said, 'We were not put here to make each other miserable.'"

Thanks Patt and everyone else who took the time to share your thoughts.

Maybe there is no clear-cut answer to the question. Maybe there is no definitive line between what we *can* do and what we *should* do. But I think if we keep our hearts soft and our eyes open, we will find that opportunities for both kindness and citizenship come frequently and reap big rewards for everyone involved.

"She says she wants to give people 'a little sunshine in their lives!'"

Kindness Heals, One Bead at a Time

Children's hearts are precious. They love big, forgive quickly and are incredible readers of the emotions around them. Sort of like a magnet, they attract the feelings of others and wear them as their own.

Sometimes that's good and sometimes that's bad. It can be bad when it locks up the mind in fear and confusion, but it's incredibly beautiful when it opens the door to compassion and understanding.

A woman from North Dakota named Bonnie Lund was going through a health crisis at the same time a family from her church was taking on their own battle. The family had been praying for Bonnie, and thanks to the heart of a little girl, that's right where kindness bloomed.

"I'd like to share a little kindness story about a young friend of mine named Aleksia. She is 11. Last fall I was diagnosed with thyroid cancer and I had surgery in December.

While all this was going on, Aleksia and her family were in Minneapolis as her brother, Arlyn, age 7 at the time, was fighting for his life. He had undergone a liver transplant and spent the next seven months at the Children's Hospital recovering and rebuilding his health.

He was a healthy young boy before his mysterious liver failure last July.

His parents and baby sister, who was born just before Arlyn's transplant, stayed with him in the hospital while Aleksia stayed nearby with her grandparents at the Ronald McDonald House.

During this time, Aleksia said she saw so many kids in the hospital whose parents weren't there with them and some whose parents were there, but the families were sad. She was grateful that her family could be together, but she wanted to help the other families be happy so she started 'Aleksia's Beaded Blessings.'

Through her Beaded Blessings initiative, when she hears of someone who is going through a medical challenge, she looks up the colors that represent their medical problem and makes them a bracelet or keychain and prays for them while making it. She says she wants to give people 'a little sunshine in their lives!'

She made me a beautiful bracelet with the colors for thyroid cancer: pink, blue and teal.

As I wear it, I remember her kindness and the great courage and strength her family showed through Arlyn's ordeal.

I am happy to say God is helping Arlyn heal. He is back playing soccer!"

Bonnie, the recipient of Aleksia's bracelet who shared this story is also on the mend.

Little Black Dresses Bring Joy During Trials

The hardest thing to do when I'm feeling down is the one thing I know will help me feel better. It's not exercise or sleep or eating healthier meals.

It's kindness.

I know when I'm at my worst, I have to get my eyes off myself and put them squarely on the needs of others.

It works. Every time.

But it doesn't just work for me. A Fargo, North Dakota woman says she was facing a difficult time when the perfect opportunity for kindness was born out of a short chat at a hospital coffee counter.

"For several years I have looked at the darling 'little black dresses' for baby girls at our hospital's gift shop. They have ruffle bottoms and cute headbands. I have always wanted to buy one with the hopes of having a granddaughter, but after three grandsons, I realized it may never happen.

My husband was hospitalized for a lengthy time over Christmas and New Year's this past year. Many trips were made to see him.

One day I stopped at the coffee shop in the hospital and was in line behind a young couple. The man ordered coffee for the two of them, adding 'no caffeine for my wife' which prompted the barista to ask her if she was expecting. The young wife started to cry and told her they had twin daughters in the NICU that they were leaving for the first time.

Of course that gave me the chance to ask her about the twins, learning their names, how much they weighed and how early they were. I could only say how hard it must be to leave their little ones for the first time. I squeezed her arm and told her everything would be OK.

They got their coffees and left. I got my coffee and went next door to the gift shop. Finally I could buy two of the little black dresses! The clerk helped me wrap the dresses and I wrote the twins' names on the bag. I brought the bag to the NICU and left it with a nurse explaining I didn't know the parents but I knew the names of the twins.

A couple days later I was going up the elevator to visit my husband when a young woman squeezed my arm and said, 'Thank you for the dresses.' She told me how it gave them so much joy to hang the dresses on the girls' bassinets.

I was so caught off guard but I wish I could have told her how much joy it brought to me during her sad time as well as my own difficult time.

My husband recovered fine and I hope the girls went home sooner than expected. It is true that there is joy in our sadness."

When we take our eyes off our own pain long enough to see the pain of others, there is healing for all of us.

Kindness Eases the Pain of Saying Goodbye to a Father

My friend's father-in-law recently died. It came on suddenly. It wasn't supposed to happen that way. They weren't prepared. I wonder, when it comes to losing someone we love, if we're ever really prepared.

The hole that's left while we are mourning seems like an endless chasm, and yet it's the perfect size for kindness. Kindness shown through phone calls, flowers, shared memories and stories that come to life only after the living are gone.

My friend says she and her family were tremendously blessed by one of those stories, sent from a man they had never met.

"Yesterday morning before we left for the funeral, my husband received an email from his mother, sharing a comment made on the newspaper website in conjunction with the obituary. I guess comments and photos may be uploaded onto their site for the family to view, just as it is on the funeral home's site. The following comment was left:

'I only met Larry once in my life, when I was a 12-year-old boy who loved trains. Larry was working in Jackson, Ohio, and was kind enough to give my brother and me a ride in the locomotive as he and the crew switched the yard, back in 1983. I remember him as a kind man. He sure created a lasting memory with me; giving a young rail fan a ride in the cab! My dad took a picture of us with Larry the next morning before he left with the train back to Springfield. I saw a posting about Larry's death and I thought his face looked familiar from the picture I had.

My sympathies for your loss.'

The kindness that my father-in-law showed this man when he was a young boy was typical of the man Larry was. He would show kindness but never ask for accolades to accompany it. No one ever knew of this kindness until he passed. This was such a precious memory for our family to receive.

In my mind, Larry's kindness was not the only one exhibited. The second came from the man who left this story. He did not have to go onto the site and share this memory. As a matter of fact, how often do people shy away from doing exactly that simply out of embarrassment or lack of time? Yet, our family could not have asked for a more precious gift in a time of need. My husband's mother even printed the story and photo out and had it sitting on a table by the casket, showing how very much this meant to her and the family.

To me, kindness is God's love walking itself out through the hands and feet of His people. This man was certainly God's hands and feet to our family during this time of saying goodbye."

Kindness can't take away the pain, but even in the smallest doses, it does act as a powerful balm until we are able to find our balance once again.

When We Talk, Then Do, Kindness Becomes Contagious

Walt Disney once said, "The way to get started is to quit talking and begin doing."

That works well for amusement parks, but it also works well in the realm of kindness.

Alicia Stewart is a mom who feels frustrated with the way girls sometimes treat each other. When she saw it happening in her daughter's second-grade classroom, she decided to put together a retreat for girls that would focus on their self-esteem and compassion toward others.

She is done talking and ready to begin "doing," and as Alicia excitedly shared with me, the lessons she is preparing for the school are already having an impact in her own home.

"I finally had a discussion with my kids and told them what I am planning.

We talked about how mean girls can be to each other and how we are going to attempt to change that. The first thing my daughter said was, 'Thank you so much! That is going to make my life so much easier!'

A couple days later my son, Chancie, came home from school waving a bag in his hand yelling 'Look what I got for Alex! Look what I got for Alex!'

Alex is a boy in his class that he has mentioned on numerous occasions.

Chancie told us one of his fifth-grade teachers often has to give him string as a belt to hold his pants up and has bought him sweatpants in the past.

Chancie was also upset one day when he felt like another teacher was playing favorites. When two boys asked the same question, Alex got in trouble while the other student did not.

Well, my son noticed Alex's shoes were loose and flapping on the bottom and giving him blisters because they were too small. Chancie wanted to give him his old (but still very nice) shoes, but Alex didn't wear that size. He asked Alex what size shoes he wears and what his favorite color is. With the help of Chancie's granny, who brings him home every day, Chancie bought Alex a brand new pair of shoes!

He was so excited to take them to him at school. With the help of his teacher, Alex got the shoes without the whole class knowing. Alex told Chancie they were the best shoes he has ever had!

Chancie says the conversation we had about kids (mostly girls) not being kind to each other was what inspired him to give Alex new shoes."

Talking that leads to doing can create an excitement for kindness that is contagious and just might mean a making few new friends.

Teenage Boys Chip Away at Kindness

I really should have kept a list of all the people who helped me during my battle with breast cancer. It would be filled with the names of family and friends who delivered meals and picked up kids and sent cards.

But it would also be filled with the names of strangers who helped me get through each day after my surgery when I was desperate to return to my routine.

Friendly people seemed to come out of nowhere when I needed them most. Just like the two boys who helped my friend Teresa when she was dealing with a painful rib injury.

"This past week I needed to make my normal trip to our local grocery store. Truthfully, I really enjoy these trips. Many, many times I enjoy being a helping hand.

I have joked with friends that I really should go to the manager and ask for a job. I love helping bewildered men find the things on the list that their wives have sent them there to buy. Or those with failing eyesight to read a label. Or others who may not be able to read a recipe a friend gave them. I have moved carts from awkward places, bagged groceries to help out a very stressed employee, and listened to many grocery checkers who just seem to think I have a warm smile and a caring ear.

But recently I was the one who was helped. You see, several weeks ago I cracked a rib from a silly fall. I have been healing nicely but the grocery store was one place I needed to be a bit careful.

I was in the snack aisle looking for our favorite chips when I spotted the very last bag way back on an upper shelf. I tried a couple of times to reach it, but stretching above my head is still the thing that brings the most pain from my sensitive rib. I placed one foot on the lower shelf and tried again but still no success. I figured I'd need to skip the chips.

Then, out of the blue, came two sweet teenage boys. The older one asked, 'Do you need some help?' I was startled, but then said, 'Why, yes, I sure do' with a big smile on my face.

The young man climbed right up on that lower shelf and reached way back and pulled out the last bag in the store. Hallelujah! I took the bag, thanked them, and told them they had done their Random Act of Kindness for the day. They smiled and walked away.

What blessed my heart was that they were not walking through the store in their own little self-absorbed worlds. They were not on their phones or sulking because mom had asked them to go pick up something from the store.

Really, I was very unnoticeable with my dilemma, yet they paid attention and offered to help a stranger. Maybe it was a little thing for them, but it was a big thing for me. I'm sure you can tell, we really like those chips!"

Chips and kindness: That sounds like the perfect combination!

Kindness Changes the Way You See

One of the great lessons cancer taught me was the importance of getting my thought-life in order.

There are way too many things in this world that could go wrong. If we allow ourselves to think whatever thought pops into our heads, we risk being dragged into a black hole of despair.

But how do we replace those negative thoughts with something more positive? What do we think about instead?

Kindness.

It's been my secret weapon for the past six years, and I've discovered I'm not the only one using it. JoAnne Vieweg of Fargo, North Dakota has also uncovered the beauty that comes from looking at life through the lens of kindness.

"When I first discovered I had breast cancer 10 years ago, I was truly worried about the impact on my family, especially my grandson with whom I share a very close bond.

A year ago, a second unrelated cancer was discovered. It was treated quickly and effectively, however that diagnosis took me right back to the overpowering feelings I had experienced a decade before.

Suddenly the world felt very ominous and threatening. I worried daily about the safety and welfare of my family.

Then kindness came to my rescue.

One day, I found myself aggravated with a person at a drive-thru when I ordered a soda. I asked if they had caffeine free diet. He said they had diet and that it was probably caffeine free. He didn't really know, but assured me it was okay.

I went ahead and ordered it anyway knowing that I could tolerate a bit of caffeine, but felt aggravated with him that he did not know for sure. By the time I reached the window to pay, he had checked with his manager and discovered it was not caffeine free. He apologized and offered two other choices I might make instead.

I suddenly found myself no longer aggravated. I was pleased he had gone above and beyond and sought out answers. Not only that, he offered other options.

I realized that noticing his kindness made me feel happier and pleased with the world. I decided to watch out for kindnesses around me every day. The person in line at the checkout who let someone go ahead; the driver who patiently let the other car go first; the toddler who picked up her friend's dropped toy and returned it rather than keeping it herself.

This has helped me see the world in a friendlier light and has helped ease my distress and sense of foreboding. The world can indeed be a bright and welcoming place."

It's true, whether you are doing good things for others or an observant witness, kindness can change the way you see the world.

Pizza Pizza Served with a Side of Kindness

"Whoa! People work this early in the morning?"

That was my first-grade son's reaction as we passed a garbage truck recently at 5:30 a.m.

We were heading out on a family vacation. The men in the truck were hustling in the rain to pick up bin after bin of trash.

"Yes. And I'm grateful they do. How about you?" I responded.

That led to a brief conversation about many other things people do to earn money to support themselves and their families.

I could tell my son had been taking for granted that certain things just get done without thinking about who actually does them.

I have to admit, I've been guilty of that myself.

Earning a living isn't always easy or fun. With so many thankless and overlooked jobs out there, it feels especially precious when someone stops to notice a job well done. Or when the person doing the job reaches out even further to extend the hand of kindness.

A West Virginia couple was especially touched when a man working on the side of the road stopped what he was doing to acknowledge the pain they felt the day of their mother's funeral.

In an effort to thank him, the couple posed a question to their social media circle.

"Can anyone please tell us the employee's name that works at Little Caesars on the south side of Parkersburg, West Virginia who stands outside dancing with the sign? He is an amazing person and incredibly respectful! We want to make sure he gets recognized for his kindness.

"As most of you know, we lost our wonderful mother, Rose, this past week. The funeral was on Saturday. This gentleman was working, and as the funeral procession passed by him, he removed his hat, placed his hand over his heart and bowed his head in honor of a woman that he'd never met! This meant the world to those of us who loved her. It touched our hearts deeply!"

What followed on Facebook was beautiful. Person after person commented, everything from "He's a cool dude!" to "He has been doing that for years."

Someone else said "He did this for my dad, too. We went in and told them about it. It is an awesome thing he does."

Nearly a dozen people had separate but similar stories of the man who stands on the side of the road, energetically encouraging people to pick up a pizza, while also giving them a side of kindness.

Starstruck Kid Finds Kindness at the Dinner Table

Every once in awhile, Saul and I play "Who would you most like to have dinner with?"

Jimmy Buffett is high on Saul's list. Mother Teresa is high on mine. I imagine we're both out of luck.

A little boy in Fargo, North Dakota will long remember a recent meal he got to share thanks to a side helping of kindness. His grandfather, Harvey Laabs, sent me this story.

"My grandson, Ethan, is a sports fanatic. At age 10, he already plays basketball in the winter, baseball in the summer and flag football in the fall. He also loves to watch sporting events, especially the West Fargo Sheyenne Mustangs High School basketball and Fargo Force hockey games. He can tell anyone who wants to listen what number any of the Timberwolves, Vikings, Wild or Twins players wear. He has plenty of heroes among these teams.

My niece, Amy, has a son name K'Andre. K'Andre is 17 years old and is a member of the USA U17 hockey team. This is a team of young men who are part of the USA Hockey's National Team Development Program.

The team was recently in Fargo to play a pair of games against the Fargo Force. Of course, Ethan and his family were there for both games. After the Saturday game, Amy led us down into the 'belly of the arena' to wait for K'Andre. During our short visit, K'Andre signed a puck for Ethan.

Ethan was beaming.

Even though it was after 10 p.m., the team was headed to a restaurant for a late dinner. Amy invited us to join her since she planned to go there as well. After K'Andre finished eating with his teammates, he came to our table and joined us.

Ethan quickly changed the seating arrangement so that he was sitting next to K'Andre. He took the children's placemat, and the two of them played tic-tac-toe. When Ethan won two out of three, K'Andre was suitably impressed. They continued on with a word find game, and ended up quizzing each other on 'What number does (insert sports star's name) wear?' Again, K'Andre was impressed with Ethan's knowledge.

All of this seems simple enough, but here was a 17-year-old young man treating this 10-year-old boy as a peer. The 'hero' was treating the 'hero-worshipper' as an equal. He was so casual about it, it wasn't as though he was going out of his way to be kind; he was just being who he is.

This is something that Ethan will remember for a lifetime; those of us that witnessed it will also remember."

Sometimes we save our best selves for a person who impresses us or for someone from whom we can benefit. A beautiful act of kindness unfolds when we remember that everyone, especially those who look up to us, deserve our time and attention.

Kindness Fills Memory of Flood Survivor

Twenty years ago this month, people along the Red River in Minnesota, North Dakota and Southern Manitoba experienced the worst flood of the area since 1826.

Homes and businesses were destroyed. Lives were swept up in a torrent of emotional and financial ruin. An entire geographic area was collectively exhausted.

Yet, when the river finally returned to its banks, along with a path of destruction, we discovered a trail of kindness.

Laura Carley of Fargo, North Dakota vividly remembers the smell that permeated the house when her basement fuel tank filled with flood water.

She remembers learning for the first time that a pool table could float.

And she remembers the people who showed up in her time of need.

"In 1957 my family home was destroyed by the tornado that went through Fargo, and 40 years later, in 1997, my family home was hit by a flood.

It is hard to think back on that time period without thinking of the many people who stepped up for us as we tried to keep back the river.

We lived south of Fargo and were outside of the city limits, so the process of obtaining sand and sandbags was up to each homeowner.

However, once the word got out that we needed people to help build the dike, volunteers came from all over. They would use up the sand we had and then move on to another house. When we had more sand, there always seemed to be a new parade of people who would help fill and place the bags.

The Salvation Army came by with sandwiches and drinks, friends made sure food appeared in our kitchen along with paper plates to eat it on. Thinking back on the process, it was nothing short of amazing.

Ultimately, our dike collapsed. Needless to say we were devastated.

Thankfully a mentor of mine advised me to take the time to mourn the loss of our house and taught me to open up to the kind people who wanted to help. Until you need it, you have no idea how hard it is to accept help from others. We were used to offering a helping hand, not reaching out for one.

We learned a lot as a community throughout that flood event, but the biggest lesson was the huge hearts filled with kindness that people in this area have.

Twenty years later, I still use my Red Cross cleaning bucket for flowers every April and make certain we give to both the Salvation Army and the Red Cross so they can continue to help in times of trouble."

In the minds of many people, words like "Fargo," "Grand Forks" and "April" bring to mind other words like "sandbag," "river" and "flooding." But thankfully, they also bring to mind the faces of friends and strangers who calmed the storm with kindness.

Sweet Ways to Show Kindness

I was at a Weight Watchers meeting this morning. Don't ask. The wheels fall off the bus pretty quickly when you live in a family who loves to celebrate track meets, baseball games and good grades with ice cream. Easter baskets don't seem to help the problem either.

Anyway, I was sitting in the meeting listening to the celebrations and challenges the other members were sharing when one woman brought up an interesting predicament.

"Clearly my husband doesn't understand this whole weight loss thing," she started, "because he keeps buying me chocolate."

She went on to say that for years, her husband has kept her well stocked with York Peppermint Patties. It's her favorite candy and he knows it. So he buys her a big bag every time it appears she's getting low.

It's an act of kindness, a show of love between a husband and wife who have been together a very long time.

I sat silently in my seat thinking about the beauty of that little action her husband takes. It might be worth the calories to know that my husband was at the grocery store and thought of something that would make me smile.

Oh wait, actually my husband does that. He knows I love Ben and Jerry's, so every once in a while, he will come home from a stealth trip to the grocery store and proudly present me with a pint of New York Super Fudge Chunk.

The love I feel through my husband's act of kindness is even more delightful and satisfying than the actual ice cream.

But the actual ice cream is pretty awesome as well.

Did I mention we have an issue with ice cream in our house?

Back to the meeting. As I was contemplating the loveliness of love, another woman spoke up with a possible solution.

"My husband used to buy me those too!" she said. "Once I started watching my weight, I asked him to keep the bag and just give me three a day. At some point, each day, I'd walk into the kitchen and see three little peppermint patties sitting on the counter."

It was a tiny gift, a tiny show of big love and support for her hard work each and every day. And somehow, quietly, magically, it became part of her individual love story.

I was so touched by those acts of kindness that I just had to share them with you. Perhaps candy isn't the way to go. Maybe the ice cream needs to stay in the freezer section. But I bet there are more ways to love the people in our lives than we ever pause to recognize. And I bet there are more ways that the people in our lives are already loving us that we fail to see.

I hope your eyes are opened by this casual conversation just like mine were. There is something so sweet about kindness, whether it involves chocolate and ice cream or not.

I wanted to pull them all close, break through their mountain of insecurities and say, "Do you want to know what really matters, what will continue to matter 30 years from now?
Kindness."

Kindness is the Most Important Muscle

I didn't think time travel was possible until I was sitting at a track meet the other night. It was my daughter's very first meet. I thought it would be my very first meet too.

I was told ahead of time that it would be a test of endurance — not for the student athletes, but for their parents. In anticipation of the four-hour event, I brought along my chair-in-a-bag, a football and a thermal tote full of snacks for my younger boys. I found the perfect spot in the sun to settle in and watch the action.

I wasn't sitting there 10 minutes when I started having flashbacks.

All of a sudden, I was 13 years old again.

I remembered being in awe of the amount of kids all in one place. And the cute boys from the other schools. And feeling so grown up because I had taken a bus with my team and had money for the concession stand in my drawstring bag.

The races didn't go so well for my seventh grade self. I fell over the hurdles, nearly dropped the baton during the relays and almost took off a coach's head with the discus. But I sure had fun in an anxious, on-the-brink-of-adulthood way.

This wasn't my first track meet. It was just my first track meet as a parent. How could I have forgotten?

As I watched the girls giggle at the boys and the kids from various teams bravely congratulate each other, I thought about what else I felt at that age: stuck in time.

I couldn't understand that my choices today would affect my tomorrow. Or that in another 10 years, the pimples and bad haircut and bruised knees wouldn't matter.

I wanted to call over each girl individually and tell her she was beautiful and talented and smart. I wanted to assure her that even if she couldn't see her own gifts yet, they were there. They would continue to quietly develop just below the surface until someday everyone would see her true inner exquisiteness.

I wanted to pull them all close, break through their mountain of insecurities and say, *Do you want to know what really matters, what will continue to matter 30 years from now?*

Kindness.

Do you want to know how to survive this awkward interval? How to truly win friends and influence people?

Kindness.

It's so simple. Yet, I struggled with it mightily at that age and sometimes I still do.

I'm so glad my daughter joined the track team, because if she hadn't, I never would have gotten to travel through time.

Perhaps I would have forgotten forever that the most important muscle to develop is the one that continually leads us to be kind.

Teacher's Letter Home Shows Great Kindness

My friend who is a teacher showed me a very funny poster. It has pictures of two owls. One owl is looking wise and well-tailored in his round glasses and cap. The other owl looks like a deranged lunatic with a torn shirt and frayed feathers.

The caption on the poster says, "Teachers at the beginning of the school year" and "Teachers at the end of the school year."

As a classroom volunteer, I've had the privilege of seeing students up close all year long. I have to say, when spring is in the air, something strange happens to those little bodies.

A new boisterous energy makes them want to run and play and laugh, but does not make them want to learn reading, writing or arithmetic.

This puts teachers in an awkward position, because they are still supposed to teach those subjects for another few months.

It's easy to get dragged down into the chaos, which for control-freaks like me, often means grasping at anger and negativity instead of focusing on the positives.

My friend Mary got a lovely letter from her daughter's sixth grade teacher, who is not only seeing the good in this unique time of year, but is also taking the time to comment on it.

"I would like you to know just how much I appreciate having your daughter in my classroom.

She always tells me 'Thank you' at the end of class with a smile on her face. Her kind words keep me going at the end of a sometimes long day. Her class can be a bit on the excitable side, which means they get a stern talking to quite frequently, but Betsy is such a positive and kind example for her classmates to follow."

Mary, Betsy's mom, says, "Betsy's words at the end of class are sometimes what the teacher needs to push her through the day. The teacher's words to Betsy, my husband and me were equally important. That letter made us smile and put a little spring in our step. Kind words can go a long way, and pick you up when you just feel like you want to cry."

When a teacher shows such kindness outside of the classroom by writing a letter like this, you can bet there are some pretty great things happening inside her classroom as well. And it sure is nice to know that some of the students take the time to recognize it and say thank you.

Everything Changes When Kindness Enters the Room

How is it that things can look so drastically different based on our ever-changing outlook?

Like the little park bench that's tucked along a pebble path and surrounded by colorful blossoms. It looks so quaint and inviting, until that becomes the place where your boyfriend chooses to dump you.

Then it looks rusty and worn out and covered in bird poop.

Some things that are beautiful become less captivating, but as Diana Anderson of West Fargo, North Dakota found out, it also works in reverse. A nice evening can become magical when kindness enters the room.

Here's her story:

"On New Year's Eve we went to dinner with my husband's family. We had not all been together since the passing of his dad, Wally, four years ago. We were a group of 12 and we had a wonderful meal at Granite City in Fargo. After many laughs, great food and drinks, it was time to move the party to our house.

Our attentive waitress informed us that someone had paid our bill. We all were stunned and thought it was just a silly prank at first.

We looked at each other and then around the restaurant to see if this was in fact really happening.

The restaurant was still abuzz with people laughing, eating and enjoying the night. Patrons were entering the restaurant while others were leaving. Employees were bringing food and drinks to tables. The scene was the same as it had been when we entered the restaurant just an hour earlier and yet it was completely different. It is amazing how it changed the mood of the rest of the night, and how all of a sudden, we could see the kindness and smiles radiating around us.

The 12 of us pooled every bit of cash we had and gave it to the server. Our waitress was so surprised and grateful. I'm not sure how much we gave her, but she deserved every penny she made.

Each individual family at our table, all 5 of them, committed to paying for another family's meal in the future. I'm not sure if the rest of them have followed through yet, but the next night my husband and I took our kids to Red Lobster and had so much fun choosing another family to bless."

Do you need to change the atmosphere around you? Perhaps you want to consider bringing kindness into play.

Kindness Replaces Some of the Madness in March

A whole new language arises during the month of March in the house of a college basketball coach.

We use words like "seed" and "bracket" in daily conversation, but even more curious, in my house at least, is the way my husband begins to use the word, "March."

In the midst of a tight game on TV, Saul will yell out things like, "It's getting awfully Marchy in here!" or "It smells like March!"

I've even heard him say, "I'm feeling Marchy." That one makes me a little nervous.

It's sort of like living in a land of Smurfs. It's Smurftastic!

Only sometimes March isn't Smurftastic. Sometimes it's edgy and tense and filled with a roller coaster of emotions that take you up and down, up and down.

That's what makes March so Marchy. And it happens to every coach's wife out there.

We all get a little jittery, a little too tuned into ourselves and our team.

The wives of the basketball staff at South Dakota State have found a way to combat these symptoms. Between the eight women, they have 10 kids, two babies on the way, and more than 30 years of combined March Madness experience.

Alicia Henderson is one of those coaches' wives. In an effort to have some fun and keep the games in perspective, she and the other wives have put an interesting spin on March.

"Our staff here at SDSU has decided to start something fun in the month of March to get people excited about the tournaments, March Madness, and the Final Four.

For my birthday in December, I started a totally fun tradition two years ago of picking up a friend or two and driving through a couple of drive thrus and paying it forward by paying for the car behind us! Alison and Erin (the head coach's wife and director of operations' wife) joined me this year.

Fast forward to Feb. 14. Alison stopped at Starbucks to pick up Valentine cookies for her twins' preschool teachers. Someone had left $15 for the next customer to use and that person was Alison!

She texted me after and questioned whether I had just been at Starbucks and left the money. It wasn't me, but it got us thinking about doing something fun with our staff to build a little camaraderie going into tournament time.

An initial thought was to do a group dinner and pay for the table next to us, but immediately it turned to 'let's get as many people as we can to join us in spreading kindness' and March Kindness became that thing.

We had a road game and the staff wives got together to watch, and we told them our idea. From there the fun really began. Everyone from the coaches' wives to our radio guy's wife to our trainer's girlfriend was super excited and totally on board!

So literally a complete stranger did a random act of kindness at a Starbucks in Brookings, South Dakota, and a group of women (who I think are pretty amazing and have been there for me during the tough days of this crazy profession) embraced the idea of spreading kindness during a stressful/busy tournament time!

We have been doing random acts almost daily. Our only hope is that this will continue to spread and become a yearly tradition each March, no matter our paths in this crazy coaching world!"

The women printed notecards to hand out when they do an act of kindness that say "March Kindness" and list the social media links and hashtags so others can get involved too.

You can join the March Kindness movement on instagram @marchkindness, twitter @marchkindness17, or facebook.com/marchkindness.

'Neighbors' Columnist Gets Well-Deserved Kindness

I am about to rat out my fellow columnist. In a good way, of course.

Bob Lind has been writing the Neighbors column in the *Fargo Forum* since before I was born.

Just kidding.

But he has been writing it for quite a while, right around 20 years in fact.

His words introduce us to the people, places and things that are right under our noses that we sometimes forget to see. He helps us solve mysteries, like *Who is Olga?* and charms us with delightful anecdotes like the *Unexpected Valentine Moment* in a fast-food parking lot.

While many of us love his witty writing style, I'm certain anyone who knows Bob can truly see what lies behind each column he writes. Bob has a heart for people.

Bob was one of the first people to email me after I began writing the *Kindness is Contagious* column back in 2011. His words gave me confidence and confirmed that I was on the right track.

Since then, several times a year, Bob's name will pop up in my inbox. Each email delivers the words of a professional encourager: "Nicole, nice, nice column again today. Keep those kindness things rolling!" or "Nicole, your column today was tremendous."

The kindness of those emails means more than I could ever express. So when I read Bob's most recent letter, I knew I had to share it as proof that what goes around, comes around.

"Nicole,

Here's your old fellow columnist with a yarn out of Fargo. Not seeking publicity, but when this happened, I of course thought of you.

The other day, I came home from somewhere with lots of stuff to carry into the house. But first, I decided to check to see if we had mail. I laid everything, including my car/house keys, on the trunk of my wife's car in our garage.

I got our mail, picked up everything (I thought) I'd piled on the other car and went into our house.

A while later, my wife, Marcie, took off in her car.

Several blocks from our house, she stopped at a red light. Immediately, some guy came running up and dangled some keys outside her window. She recognized them as being my keys.

Apparently this dumb husband of Marcie's had left my keys on her trunk. Somewhere, they'd fallen off as she was driving, and this guy had seen it, stopped, picked them up, and caught up with her at the red light to give them to her.

What a miracle they hadn't been lost forever.

And what a great guy, to go to the trouble of returning them to Marcie.

Nicole, back here in your and Saul's town of Fargo, kindness and thoughtfulness live on.

Keep those columns coming, Nicole."

Yep, Bob Lind is one special guy, and I'm grateful for his encouragement. I'm also glad that good guys like him catch a break once in a while when they leave their keys on their wives' trunks.

You can find Bob Lind's Neighbors column every Monday, Tuesday and Thursday in *The Forum of Fargo-Moorhead*.

Netflix Series Sparks Ideas for Kindness

A strange thing is happening. The kids are fed, the dishes are done (sort of) and the couch begins calling my name. Actually, it's not the couch that's drawing me in, it's the television.

Ahhh, Netflix.

I've always admired the beauty of being able to watch what you want when you want it, but at the risk of sounding like an 80-year-old woman, I don't think most of what's on TV these days is worth watching. And certainly not with my kids in the room.

However, I stumbled upon a new reality series the other day that makes binge watching seem almost as important as exercising. It's called *The Kindness Diaries*, and it's based on a book by the same name.

Here's the gist: a former stockbroker named Leon quits his day job in search of a meaningful life. He sets out across the globe on a canary-colored vintage motorcycle relying totally on the kindness of strangers for shelter, food and gas.

The episode I watched last night featured a homeless man named Tony sharing his underwear with Leon.

Tony owns so few material things, yet he was willing to share them with a total stranger. Leon spent the night on Pittsburgh's cold concrete with Tony.

The next morning, Leon had a surprise. I won't give it away just in case you want to watch it for yourself.

The beauty of the show is that it reminds me there are ways to love our neighbors that we may have never considered. And the exchange that happens in the space where kindness lives leaves both people feeling like they were the recipient of a huge blessing.

A woman in northern Minnesota sent me a letter about some very interesting work she's done over the years in the name of kindness. Some of it is off the beaten path, but some of it isn't. Thanks to her perspective, she's come out of each situation feeling like she was the one being given the greater gift.

"For years I provided emotional and practical support to persons living with AIDS in San Francisco. I know that John appreciated his laundry being done every week, and I will carry with me forever the remembrance of the smile on his face as I put his clean clothes back on his closet shelves. It was so worth those three flights of stairs up and down to the laundry room every Saturday morning.

I currently volunteer at the local library, shelving books in the kids' section. The connections and conversations I've had with library staff mean so much more to me than knowing books got put in their proper places.

All is neat and tidy in the kids' section of the library when I finish each Thursday, and I leave feeling validated, appreciated and part of something bigger than myself.

I also volunteer at the local hospital, rocking babies born with drugs in their tiny systems. I whisper in the ears of those wee babes in the nursery, telling them they can grow up to be warriors, strong and brave, and I hope they will remember that they were deeply loved in that rocking chair.

I know the nurses appreciate my time and energy, and I know the stimulation is helpful for the babies in withdrawal.

But I know for sure that I am gaining tenfold of what I am giving. Rocking is peaceful, practically meditative, and knowing I am part of the solution is such a tremendous feeling.

My remembrances of doing laundry, holding hands and making cookies with a 4-year-old whose mama didn't have the energy to stand at the kitchen counter, have provided me with a lifetime of golden moments."

Are you looking for more meaning in your life? Give kindness (and maybe Netflix) a try.

You can learn more about Leon Logothetis and his real-life adventures in "The Kindness Diaries" on Netflix and on Facebook at https://www.facebook.com/leonlogothetis/.

Well-Timed Letter Reminds Me to Look for Kindness

I went to visit my father recently. He had a stroke about 9 months ago and is now a permanent resident in an assisted living facility.

He hasn't yet regained the use of the right side of his body, so he relies heavily on my step-mom and his nurses to tend to his every need.

Every several months I have the opportunity to travel from Ohio to Wisconsin to see him. Each time I go, my heart breaks at the thought of leaving.

Have you ever had that feeling? It seems like it's almost easier to stay away because then we can go about our daily routines and pretend nothing is wrong. I can almost convince myself that my dad is out fishing for the day or sitting in his sunroom reading a good Western.

Yet, my heart longs to sit by my father's side and hold his hand and tell him how grateful I am for him.

Just before I left for my trip, I got a letter from a Fargo, North Dakota man named Don Hogenson who wanted to share his experience as a resident in a full-service retirement community.

Timing is everything. Reading Don's letter before heading to see my dad made me look at the people in my father's life with observant and grateful eyes.

"Nicole,

The longer I live at Touchmark, the more I understand how much kindness is a part of who we are.

Acts of random kindness appear regularly in various publications. They usually happen in restaurants or grocery stores, but what I want to share is kindness in the context of a senior living community.

Let's start with a senior whose eyesight is failing. Somebody will read the dining room menu to them.

Or the senior who has arthritic hands and has difficulty with using various instruments. A friend is there to help them.

When the battery fails on a scooter, two other seniors will push the vehicle to the charging station.

Or how about helping someone move their chair closer to the table in the bingo room or spotting a number to make sure they don't miss a 'Bingo' win.

Or always encouraging their friends to get out of their apartments and socialize, which we know can increase the mental situation with seniors.

My dear wife, Carol, died shortly after we arrived at Touchmark. I was lost.

A couple days later, I wandered into the dining room and wondered where I should sit. A group of three very nice ladies asked me if I wanted to join them. I did and then had dinner with them regularly for many months. Their kindness helped me deal with my loss.

Finally, one lady encouraged me to try joining some men for dinner so I could have some 'man talk'. I took her advice and now have new male friends as well.

I could go on and on, but I think you get the drift. Kindness can be part of our nature if we allow it. It is good for the recipient and good for the soul.

If you want to see kindness in action, spend a few days at a senior living facility."

Thanks to Don's letter, this time when I went to visit my father, instead of seeing wheelchairs and oxygen machines, I saw people. I saw people visiting with new friends and reminiscing about old ones.

My heart was lighter than usual when I left because I know my dad is in good hands. He has people *to* care for him and people *who* care for him. And if you've got friendship and kindness in your life, what else do you need?

Dealing with Difficult People is Easier with Kindness

Remember the old *National Enquirer* magazine commercials? "Inquiring minds want to know. I want to know."

I talk about the health benefits of giving and how awkward situations can be smoothed out with kindness, but the more opportunities I have to speak in public and get immediate feedback from those messages, the more I realize I'm getting it wrong.

Well, maybe not totally wrong. It's just that I've been missing a key element in the equation. There are inquiring minds out there and they all want to know the same thing. "How do I deal with difficult people?"

Every post-presentation Q & A session contains at least one question about a nagging boss, a meddling mother-in-law or a friend who is never satisfied with the situation.

The scenario is different each time, but every single person in the audience leans in a little closer to hear the answer, because they're dealing with difficult people too.

I gotta say, if I had a go-to, no fail, do this sort of answer, I would be on a world tour right now with a best-selling book. Difficult people are hard to pin down because they're ... well, difficult.

I do have some thoughts though, based on what's worked and hasn't worked in my own life.

I think first we need to determine, what is a difficult person? Oh wait, you already know that. We all do. It's the person who makes us hesitate when we see their name come across our cell phone. Or groan when we turn into the wrong aisle at the supermarket. Or fidget with self-consciousness when we walk into a room.

Now you're not going to like what I'm about to say, but I think it's important that we ask ourselves some serious questions. *Is she the difficult one or am I? Does everyone think he's difficult or is it just me? Could this possibly be an issue with my outlook? Perhaps something rooted in jealousy, pride or ego?*

When the issue is us and not them, it's time to have a heart-to-heart with ourselves. I've had to have some stern talks with myself about being happy for other people's successes and not jealous of them. Ouch.

Okay, let's say the other person truly is difficult and everyone knows it. What do we do then?

I find myself using the three C's: compassion, control and closure.

Compassion. Building compassion for someone can change your entire relationship. Don't believe me? My mother and I had a very tumultuous rapport for a long time. (Sorry, Mom.)

I couldn't seem to get over the feelings of abandonment left from my parents' divorce, and I blamed her. It wasn't until I started digging into my mother's past that I realized people make the decisions they make for a reason. Sometimes survival mode kicks in.

What have those tough people in your life been through? What happened to make them that way? What is it they need above anything else? You will find it much easier to greet them with kindness if you can get an idea of their backstory.

The next C is Control. Regain control of the situation by building healthy boundaries into your life. Tired, stressed, anxious? Then let the phone go to voicemail.

Certain you will come to regret taking your neighbor's children for the afternoon? Then be bold enough to stand up for yourself and say, "That's not going to work for me. Hopefully I can help you another time." Be kind to yourself first.

The final C is Closure. This is a sad one. Sometimes we have to break bridges. If a person is so difficult that they are harming your mental or physical or emotional health, you need to cut them off. It will be painful to say goodbye for a season (or forever), but it will allow you to be healthy enough to nurture the relationships in your life that produce good fruit.

I have to admit, the less difficult I become, the less difficult others seem to become. Perhaps it's because we don't gravitate toward each other anymore. If I'm not gossiping or griping, they have to find a new partner to commiserate with. Or perhaps I see them differently because I'm seeing them through the lens of compassion.

Don't get me wrong, there are still plenty of days when I have to let the phone go to voicemail, but by the time I get around to returning the call, I know I can do it with kindness.

Kindness Isn't About Them, It's About You

My husband has banned me from Amazon. Not for shopping. For reading book reviews. Specifically, my book reviews.

I wrote a book and because it was about kindness, I assumed everyone would love it. So when someone left me a two-star review, I cried. Seriously, stupid I know, but I boo-hooed for almost two days. One day for each star.

The review wasn't even all that bad. Wanna see it? Of course you do. Here you go:

"I would have enjoyed this book so much if it had been stories about people who received unexpected kindness and gifts from others. I did not expect that the stories would be told by the givers. Only my personal opinion, but kindness & generosity is reduced when 'declared,' regardless of how great a gift or small the kindness given. I hope this author feels inspired to write another book that would be from the receiver's point of view. She is a gifted writer."

I read those words and wanted to scream, "Did she even read the whole book?" But somewhere between blowing my nose for the twelfth time and growing thicker skin, I remembered something. The person who wrote that review feels the same way I felt six years ago.

When I first started writing this column, I was worried because the very first story was about me and an act of kindness I had done for someone else.

I was so concerned I was on the wrong path or in some way committing a cardinal sin that I sent the story to my pastor and asked him to read it.

He gave me the okay and the rest is history.

Sure, I try to write from both points of view: those who have done an act of kindness and those who were blessed by being the recipient.

But the truth I've come to learn since immersing myself in the study of kindness is this:

Kindness isn't about them. It's about you.

The greatest perks of kindness, the physical, mental and emotional benefits, are usually bestowed on the giver, not the receiver. It's backward, but it's the way I've seen it work in my own life and the lives of others.

We live in a world that prizes humility (probably because we don't see it very often). We feel like bragging about our generosity or thoughtfulness in some way diminishes the eternal rewards for our actions. And if we're running around yelling from the mountaintops about everything we've ever done, it probably does.

But here's the flip side: when we only talk about the recipients, we come to idolize the givers. We see them as superheroes, someone we could never be because we don't have their superpowers like time, energy and money.

By sharing what we've done and how it has enriched our lives with joy and gratitude, we make kindness contagious.

We make it look fun. We make other people want to try it. And we show them that it only takes a little sacrifice to make a big difference.

Feb. 12-18 is Random Acts of Kindness week. It's meant to be a party, both online and in real life. Here's the scoop from the Random Acts of Kindness website.

"Random Acts of Kindness week [...] is an annual opportunity to unite through kindness. Formally recognized in 1995, this seven-day celebration demonstrates that kindness is contagious. It all starts with one act — one smile, one coffee for a stranger, one favor for a friend. It's an opportunity for participants to leave the world better than they found it and inspire others to do the same."

There are all kinds of great ideas to get you started and spark your imagination at randomactsofkindness.org. You can pick your favorites, create an online profile to share with friends and encourage others to give kindness a try.

Kindness is ready to take over this nation, but we have to let people know how easy it really is. No superheroes needed.

Sometimes the
temptation to play
Finder's Keepers
takes over.

Kindness Reminds Us There Are Good People in the World

When I was in kindergarten, we had a whole lesson about what to do when you find a lost wallet. We acted out make-believe scenarios in which one of us would be the person who drops the wallet, one would be the person who finds it and another would be the officer at the police station. Funny, we never talked about taking it to the front counter of a store or leaving it at the reception desk. We always took it straight to the police station.

In our little plays, we got to peek inside the wallet. Looking at that colorful monopoly money would make our fingers tingle. Would it be okay to take a little for ourselves? No, our teacher would gently remind us. All the money needs to go back to the owner.

Thinking back on that lesson of integrity, it just seems so simple. You find something that belongs to someone else and you return it to them. But we all know, that's not always the case. Sometimes the temptation to play Finder's Keepers takes over.

A reader named Julie saw the good win out and she wanted to share her story in hopes of thanking the person who did the right thing.

"Hi Nicole,

I was having a busy afternoon driving around Fargo doing errands before meeting up with friends to see a Friday night movie.

I was at Barnes & Noble when I got a text that everyone was waiting for me at the movie theatre.

I quickly took off and connected with my friends, but when I dug in my purse for my wallet, it wasn't there. My credit cards, driver's license and about $50 in cash were missing. I had a panicky feeling, but decided it must have fallen out in my car.

After I searched my car with no luck, I concluded that it had to be at the bookstore. I drove back there hoping an employee had picked it up. When I asked if there was a lost and found, the employee asked if my name was Julie. I was so relieved to get my wallet returned fully intact!

When I inquired as to where it was found, he responded that someone found it laying in the parking lot and made the assumption that a shopper from Barnes & Noble had dropped it and brought it in for safekeeping.

I hope that 'someone' reads this story and accepts my sincere thanks. There are good people in this community and often we don't get the opportunity to thank them personally.

By the way, after all the dashing around, I was able to get seated with my friends during the last preview in time to see La La Land, the perfect movie to destress after my ordeal!

The funny thing is, I was in the checkout line at Barnes & Noble with a Buddha Board, which is a serenity board based on the Zen concept of living in the moment. When I got the text that my friends were waiting for me, I put the board back and rushed out of the store! Ironic isn't it? I'm tempted to buy a board to promote serenity as I'm scrambling around to keep my schedule!

Another bit of info: I, along with most of the friends I was meeting, am a widow. We are single gals in our young 60s uniting together to get out and have fun. We have become a good support system for each other. Some lost their husbands to long ordeals like cancer and MS whereas my husband died suddenly to a brain hemorrhage. We are all dealing with a change in our life that we didn't expect and weren't prepared for, but we find comfort in doing things together."

The kindness of a stranger not only allowed Julie to make it to the movie, but it also allowed her to share in the kindness of friendship.

Service Members Treated to First-Class Kindness

I have a confession. People in uniform make me nervous.

I'm fine with a doctor's coat or a fireman's jacket, but put a police officer's crisp navy shirt and peaked dress cap in front of me, and I get a little shaky. Maybe I have a deeply hidden guilty conscience. I've never had a bad experience with authority; it's just that I feel like my very presence is under scrutiny once I see that badge.

I used to think maybe it was the person in the uniform, but then I became friends with a man at the gym who had kids the same age as mine. We would talk about child-rearing and pizza parlors between deadlifts.

Finding out that he was a police officer didn't change our easy-going relationship. It just confirmed my belief that he was one of the good guys.

I don't run into police officers all that often, so it's not a big deal. The reason it gives me pause is because this uncomfortable feeling also happens when I cross paths with members of our Armed Forces.

Back around Veteran's Day, I was standing in line at a sandwich shop behind two men in Army uniforms. I remember thinking, "I should really pay for their lunches." But as I stood there working up the nerve to step up and hand my credit card to the cashier, I couldn't do it. I chickened out.

It was so scary to say something to these two strangers who fight for our country that I said nothing.

Just then, the cashier pulled out his own credit card and said, "Guys, I'm so grateful for the time you give for my freedom that today's lunch is on me."

Why couldn't I have done that? What's my problem? Sure, they have seen things I'll never see and possess a bravery in their hearts that I may never tap into, but under the uniform, they are just people. Scared sometimes. Lonely. In need of kindness like you and me.

A man named Lee was flying from Detroit, Michigan to Charlotte, North Carolina recently when he got a lucky break; he was upgraded to first class. In the airport, he came across a group of men in uniform. Thankfully, instead of simply thinking about what he could do to say thank you, he put his gratitude into action.

Lee's wife tells the rest of the story.

"As Lee was getting settled, he noticed a group of basic training guys that were heading back to Fort Jackson in Columbia, South Carolina. After everyone was seated, Lee made his way to the group and asked them which one of them held the lowest rank. He then asked him to take his first class seat. Two other first class passengers followed suit.

Same airplane, different seats and lives, but that one random act of kindness hopefully made those service people's day. I know Lee was thrilled. He will be embarrassed I shared, because he is all about being a low-key, from-the-heart, in-the-moment kind of guy. But I just can't help it. It makes me so very proud!

I am hoping by sharing this, we all take time to pay it forward, do a random act of kindness and decide to just be nice."

Did you catch that? Once Lee gave away his first class seat, two other people did the same. Lee's kindness was contagious. Even the flight crew was touched. Lee said he was treated to both peanuts and pretzels with a full can of Diet Coke.

The next time I'm standing in line behind a service member, in honor of Lee and the men he touched with his kindness, you can bet I'm going to be bold enough to both hand over my credit card and find the nerve to say thank you.

Kindness Leaves You with Lots to Talk About

I imagine, one day, when they're very old and can't get around quite as well as they do now, Gene Hanson and Darlene Jackson Hanson will sit next to each other and say, "Do you remember when...?"

Only there is no way they will remember it all. Not because their minds will be failing, but because of the abundant life they've lived.

Some people just live kindness. It's what they do. This couple falls into that category.

I originally got an email from Lana Schlecht, a dentist in the neighboring town, telling me about this amazing couple in Edgeley, North Dakota. "Can I throw an idea in the hat for a column? You would adore these people," she wrote. I always love learning about kind and interesting people, so I gave them a call and introduced myself.

Actually, you might know them. Gene went viral, or at least his field did when he cut a Prince symbol into his land after the singer died.

Darlene has been featured in two separate books for her business acumen. Her first husband died 30 years ago, just days after they opened an aircraft manufacturing business. Darlene picked herself up by her bootstraps and made that business into a success.

She has now sold the business, but kept the building. That's where she and Gene host coffee get-togethers every weekday morning. They've been doing it ever since the cafe closed in town. Everyone's invited and if they happen to know it's your birthday, there will probably be a cake.

If it were up to Gene and Darlene to keep both the coffee and the conversation flowing, they could share their latest acts of kindness each day and never run out of material.

Gene had a neighbor he and Darlene looked after who always said, "Give back to the community." I guess you could say they've taken that commission seriously.

In the spring and summer, the Hansons are the first ones people call when a cow goes missing. Gene hops off the mower (which he was probably doing for free for an elderly friend) and takes his plane up to get a better look.

While he's flying, he's bound to take a few aerial photos to share on Facebook. It's kind of what he's known for, other than kindness of course.

In the fall, Gene plants acres of pumpkins and squash, and Darlene makes up the goodies. Then they invite every single school child in the area to come pick out a pumpkin. The only rule is that the kids have to be able to carry their own pumpkin.

Darlene told me with a chuckle that you'd never believe how ingenious kids can get when they're trying to get the biggest pumpkin in the field on that school bus.

Wintertime is full of magical acts of kindness.

If Mr. and Mrs. Claus look familiar at the town's Christmas on Main celebration, there might be a reason.

The elderly also look forward to that time of year when they too get a visit from the pair at Manor St. Joseph, a basic care facility. The senior residents revisit their youth as they sit on Santa's lap and share their secret wishes.

Kids in the country look up to the skies, not for reindeer, but for Santa's helper in an airplane.

Gene flies over the rural parts of the community in his open cockpit plane and tosses down bags of candy. One time he threw his cellphone, but that's another story. Darlene says he really started watching what he was grabbing after that.

And how about those Christmas hams and turkeys randomly left on the doorstep? You might have a better clue now who they come from each year.

Gene and Darlene have turned a book mobile into an ice cream truck, built a Super 8 Motel to encourage people to visit their community and were instrumental in establishing the town's airport.

I could go on and on. I have pages of notes, but I'm hoping you get the point. With a little creativity and some love in your heart for the people around you, kindness can fill a life and leave you with plenty to talk about someday.

Kindness in the Benefit of the Doubt

Have you ever been driving down the street, carefully obeying the rules of the road, when all of a sudden someone cuts you off?

You're forced to hit the brakes because some madman is either driving like a bat out of Hades or didn't check his mirrors well enough to notice you were there.

How about those times you walk into the store right behind someone who lets the door flop in your face? It would have taken no effort for them to hold the handle a moment longer, but instead you're left thinking, "How rude!"

Sure, there are probably people in this world going out of their way to ruin another person's day, but most of the time, I don't think that's the case.

Most of the time, I think people just aren't thinking. Or perhaps they're thinking too hard. Maybe they are so deep in thought they aren't noticing the situation around them.

Have you ever let someone's hustle hurt you?

A woman named Debbie had an experience while grocery shopping in Mankato, Minnesota. She was in a bit of a hurry to catch up with her niece. She certainly didn't mean any offense, but I imagine the scene at the checkout could have been awkward if it hadn't been for the nice lady in front of her and Debbie's own reaction to the act of kindness.

"This past week, my niece and I bought groceries. She went to the self-checkout counter, but I told her that I never use those.

I said I prefer to wait to be served so someone has job security. The checkout lady thanked me for that comment.

The clerk finished ringing in the young lady in front of me, but there were still a few items left on the counter.

Figuring the buyer had stepped away to get another item, I asked if the worker could scan my single item quickly and showed her the cash I had in hand. The young lady in front of me stated those were still her items. I apologized for not understanding the situation. She promptly offered to buy my single item and wouldn't take no for an answer.

I told her the cash I had in my hand would be going into the Salvation Army red kettle in her honor.

I was so amazed she would add to her grocery bill for a complete stranger. Made my day!"

Now obviously, Debbie wasn't being rude or thoughtless, but thanks to everyone's temperament, a potentially uncomfortable situation instead gave way to a whole chain of kind events.

When the guy cuts me off in traffic or the woman slams the door in my face, instead of getting offended, I like to play a little game.

I ask myself, What is going on in that person's life right now?

Is he hurrying to the hospital because he just found out his wife is in labor? Is she deep in thought because she is trying to figure out how to pay for her son's new basketball shoes? Or did she spend the night taking care of her elderly mother and now she's so exhausted she can't see straight?

I'll never know the reason behind other people's behavior, but it's freeing to know that I don't have to let their actions determine my reactions.

Trying to see life through someone else's eyes reminds me that we all have our own battles to fight and the greatest kindness we can sometimes give is simply the benefit of the doubt.

Kindness Through Quiet Bags and Batman Bandaids

I'm afraid I've forgotten what it's like to have small children. How is that even possible? My kids are 12, 11 and 6. It's not like they're adults. They are definitely still in need of guidance and discipline, but life is a whole lot different (dare I say easier?) than when they were toddlers.

I see moms walking through the grocery store looking hassled and harried as a wiggly 2-year-old tries to squirm out of the cart.

I have totally been there.

I was waiting in line at Walmart the other day when a mom with two little ones struggled to get information from the clerk while her kids simultaneously tried to climb up her legs.

I felt awfully smart when I remembered I had Batman bandaids in my purse. Who would have known I could make friends so fast?

Mavis Freuh is a friend of mine from Alexandria, Minnesota. She reached out to me when I was diagnosed with breast cancer, because she had been walking the same road.

I should have known from that sweet act of support that kindness is just part of her nature. The more I get to know her, the more I realize the depth of her love for others, including those she doesn't know, like the exasperated parents who apprehensively bring their occasionally noisy children to a place where people go to find acceptance, comfort and a few moments of quiet: church.

Mavis says it was the kindness of others that originally led her to an idea that has become contagious.

"Several years ago, when my son was small, we visited family and went to church in Oakes, North Dakota.

They had 'quiet bags' for the kids, a bag with some distractions for them like a stuffed toy, coloring pages, crayons, a car and a book. Both my husband and I thought this would be a great addition to our own church.

The nursery in our hometown church wasn't 'soundproof', and we felt self-conscious of our loud toddler.

With our tax refund money, we bought cloth bags, found clearance stuffed bunnies, used coupons for Etch a Sketches and found Bible coloring books at the dollar store. I painted on each bag and we filled them up.

Over the years, someone brought in two stands to hang them on, and our boys have helped us fill and reorganize the bags.

If it makes some parents with little kids feel more welcome and more willing to stay for church with their kids, then that's great. It was our way of spreading kindness."

May we never grow so far away from our own life experiences that we forget just how challenging they were at one time, and how refreshing it felt when someone stepped in with a well-timed bandaid, a coloring book or just a smile.

I may have forgotten what it's like to have small children, but luckily, enough of them cross my path to keep me honest ... and kind.

Be the Good

What do you want to be when you grow up? I sure hope you're not one of those people who thinks they are already too old to decide. Isn't that what the new year is for? New beginnings?

I see the commercials on TV telling me I should be skinny or try a new exercise machine or buy a book to become a financially fit super parent.

All of that would be nice, but honestly, when my kids grow up, all I want them to be is kind. That's all I want to be too. Kind.

I volunteer in my son's first grade classroom once a week. I'm only there for an hour, and I never do anything that feels all that monumental, so imagine my surprise when Ben's teacher presented me with a beautifully wrapped gift.

It is a wooden sign she had created with her own hands that says, "Believe there is good in the world." Some of the letters are written in orange, so the second message, "Be the good", radiates from the artwork as well.

I cried right there in the first grade classroom when I opened it. I cried because I was touched that this teacher would take the time to make something so lovely for me, and I cried because I was honored that when she thought about people who see the good in the world, she thought about me.

I do believe there is good in the world. I believe the good is actually more abundant than the evil, but we don't see it that way because we live in a world that amplifies the darkness. We get confused and buy into the lies that this world is falling apart and we all better look out for ourselves.

But let's stop and think about that. Is hiding in our bunker really creating the legacy we are hoping for? When you're no longer here, do you want people to say, "She did a good job of making it to the gym everyday, and he always drove nice cars, but I don't know much about them, they kept to themselves"?

I imagine not.

I think we all long to do something that makes a difference. Something that may in some small way leave a footprint that says, "I was here."

Maybe that means raising compassionate children.

Maybe that means cooking a meal for a soul who hungers for a friend.

Maybe that means letting go of our wants to take care of another person's needs.

But none of that is going to happen unless we are intentional. That's why I ask what you want to be when you grow up.

Have you decided that when people think of you they are going to think of kindness? Have you decided to take one tiny step each day to make that happen?

Have you decided to give up all conversations that are filled with envy or judgement and instead only use words that breathe life into the room?

This new year, I have two wishes for you. First, I hope you begin to believe there is good in the world. And second, I pray you make the choice to be the good.

Teacher Creates Classroom of Givers

My friend was telling me a story about her son who is a freshman in college. He noticed a peer consistently walking to class without a coat. So he gave him his own.

No fanfare. No conversation or touching exchange of words as the coat was quietly laid on his desk. Just an offering that says, "I see you and I care."

I have to believe the young man receiving the coat will remember that act of kindness for the rest of his life. Maybe it will be just the nod of confidence he needs to keep on going to create a life different than he had known.

But what about my friend's son? How does that happen? How do we create kids who are not only willing to do the right thing, but actually notice the need in the first place?

I think we have to teach them to see.

That is exactly what Sheri Jordan is doing at Bennett Elementary School in Fargo, North Dakota.

She's been taking her class of fifth graders to the Great Plains Food Bank every December for the last 10 years. Parents have always stepped up in abundance as volunteer drivers.

Sheri says the experience is so impactful that many of those same parents and children go back and volunteer again with their entire families.

Our world being what it is, rules are often put in place to protect our children.

One of those new rules states that teachers can no longer use parents as drivers to transport the kids to the food bank.

No ride means no field trip.

But perhaps that rule is exactly what paved the way for extraordinary kindness.

Every year, a group of women from Fargo are invited to a holiday gathering where they party for a purpose. Each woman brings canned goods or cash donations to fill the food bank pantry.

It was at this event that Sheri ran into Tracy Green, a high school classmate and Fargo area realtor.

When Tracy heard that Sheri wasn't going to be able to take her class to the food bank this year, she offered to talk to her friend, John McLaughlin, from Valley Bus company.

John offered the bus, Tracy's realty company paid for the driver and before you know it, Sheri, 27 fifth graders and a few parent volunteers were on their way to the food bank to spread some holiday cheer.

In just one hour, those students had packed 326 backpacks for kids in North Dakota schools.

Sheri says each one of her kids left there feeling like Santa Claus:

"My students, for the most part, are from homes where their basic needs are met or exceeded.

We do have some students at Bennett Elementary who receive them, but not as many as most Fargo Elementary Schools.

The 326 backpacks that the students created are distributed on a weekly basis to students who may not have food in their homes to eat over the weekend.

It is so powerful for my students to learn that some children are living in homes with that depth of need. Children inherently want to be helpers. I witness such empowerment in them when they are given the opportunity to make a difference in another child's life.

They come back to the classroom more excited and pleased with themselves than with any other experience I have witnessed. They truly experience the joy of giving.

I think when kids can experience this feeling at a young age it plants the seed of joy in them that continues to grow throughout a lifetime.

If my students can leave my classroom having experienced kindness and the joy of giving, then I have made a difference that extends far beyond elementary school."

Thanks to some kind adults who have learned to see a need and fill it, Sheri is able to continue creating a whole new generation of givers whose kindness will ripple for years to come.

You can learn more about the Great Plains Food Bank or make a donation at www.greatplainsfoodbank.org.

Kindness Helps Us See More Clearly

You know what I love about this time of year? The Hallmark Channel. I can sit for hours watching cheesy holiday movies.

They usually involve some small town charm and an act of kindness that probably wouldn't ever happen in real life. Or maybe it would.

This story from Teresa Braaten of Wyndmere, North Dakota reminds me that every so often, Christmas miracles really do happen.

"Once upon a time, there was a boy who lost his glasses. Now, these weren't just any glasses, but very expensive, and relatively new bifocal glasses that came with a large price tag as all bifocals do.

The boy knew these glasses were special and necessary and that he needed to hold them dear. 'On your face, or in your case,' the boy's mother would remind him often.

On this particular day, however, the boy misplaced his glasses without realizing it. When he went to put his glasses on three days later, they were nowhere to be found.

'They are at school,' he confidently told his mother. 'No they're not,' said his sister indignantly. 'Well, how do you know?' the mother asked. 'He was reading when he was in the car on the way to Canada last Friday,' the sister said on Sunday evening.

'Uh, she's right,' the boy stammered.

The boy went on to explain that the last time he remembered having the glasses was when he, his two sisters and a friend stopped at a baseball field to take a break on their long drive to Canada to see relatives.

He had taken them off and set them on top of his coat while they were taking pictures.

While the boy remained calm during all of this, the mother started issuing orders like a drill sergeant: 'Search the car! Go through your bags! Search the car again! Call your cousins in Canada!'

When all of these things had been done and redone several times, the boy and his mother went to bed and slept fitfully. Where could the glasses be?

After the eyeglass-less boy went to school the next morning, the mother had an idea.

She asked the sister, 'Where was the park? Where were you when you were at the park?'

The mother then called the City Hall in Drayton, North Dakota, where the nicest young woman answered the phone and immediately took pity on what probably sounded like a deranged mother on the other end of the line.

'My son may have left his glasses in your town baseball field on Friday, and I know this is a long shot, but did anyone turn them in over the weekend?' asked the mother.

'No, they didn't,' the nice woman replied, 'but I'd be happy to go out and look for you later this morning.'

Even if the glasses were nowhere to be found, the simple fact that she had found someone so sweet and willing to assist renewed the mother's faith in humanity.

As the mother went about her errands that day, she kept telling people about the nice woman who offered to go and look for the boy's glasses.

About three hours later, the mother's cell phone rang. 'Hi. I'm calling back from the Drayton City Hall. I have good news. As I was looking around the park for your son's glasses, I ran across the banker from town eating lunch in the park. He helped me look, and he found the glasses in the middle of the baseball diamond. They must have sat there all weekend. They look like they're in perfect condition. Can I mail them back to you?' she asked.

The elated mother and her son can now be seen camping by the mailbox waiting for a very important and much anticipated priority-mail box to be delivered."

What a delightful story of kindness! If only the nice City Hall lady and the banker eating lunch would have fallen in love... I'm certain Hallmark would have come calling.

Hunger and Kindness Lead to Friendship

More often than not, when we do random acts of kindness, we never hear about it again. We don't ever truly know the impact it made on the other person. We just have to trust that kindness worked whatever magic in that person's life that was needed at that exact moment.

But every once in a while, an act of kindness will lead to a new friendship, and we get to enter the experience from another perspective.

Lori Walker, of Worthington, Minnesota sent me two letters. One is from her daughter's point of view and the other is from one of her daughter's new friends.

"My daughter, Jenny, is an Airman First Class in the United States Air Force. She is presently stationed at Travis Air Force base in Fairfield, California. She was home for two weeks this summer while doing some recruiting for the Air Force. Jenny was at the Empire Mall in Sioux Falls, South Dakota doing a recruiting exercise.

While there, she decided to take a break and have some lunch, but then realized that she did not have any money with her. She had gotten a ride to the mall with a fellow airman and had left her money in her vehicle. She sat down at one of the tables in the food court.

A short time later, a couple of girls from Iowa, Jessica and Ashley, came up to Jenny and thanked her for her service and offered to buy her lunch!

Jenny was so touched by that act of kindness that she became a little emotional.

She told them about not having any money with her and here they were thanking her for her service and wanting to buy her something to eat!

Jenny accepted, and they had a wonderful meal together and good conversation. They told Jenny that they were on their annual shopping trip to Sioux Falls. They asked Jenny questions about being in the Air Force.

Before they went their separate ways, they took a picture together and the girls asked Jenny if they could be friends on Facebook. Later that day, Jessica made a post on Facebook about their get together. I was so touched by this small act of kindness to my daughter that I felt compelled to share it with you."

Here's what Jessica posted about the interaction:

"As Ashley and I were doing our usual Sioux Falls shopping at the mall, we had a lovely experience. We had just sat down with our meals in the food court. Ten minutes into eating, a lady of service sat at a table just down from us. My first thought was to go thank her for her service, but then we decided to offer to pay for her meal. She thanked us so much and proceeded to tell us that she had forgotten her money and had not realized it until she went to buy herself some food.

She cried, which of course caused us to shed a tear or two. It is experiences like this one that make you really believe that everything happens for a reason.

Thank you so much, Jenny, for having a lovely conversation with us and teaching us so much about what you do; and a special thanks for doing what you do. It is truly amazing."

Jenny Walker will be deploying to the Middle East in January. Perhaps this expression of love in a food court will stay with her to remind her how much the people back home appreciate her sacrifice.

Kindness Overpowers Fear

When I was a freshman in college, I had a stalker.

Several of my friends were at a fast food restaurant near the University of Wisconsin campus when they saw a man sitting at a table with huge photos of me spread out in front of him.

They were confused, but knew something was very wrong with that scenario.

I would have thought it was all a joke or some kind of misunderstanding, but then the phone calls started coming. I was a local pageant title holder and the man would pretend to be a newspaper reporter calling for an interview. He never asked anything inappropriate, but he did his best to keep me on the line and find out where all of my future affairs were going to take place.

The Resident Assistant in my dorm and the rest of the people who managed the facility took quick action to keep me safe.

For the rest of the year, anytime I had a nighttime class or needed to be out past dusk alone, they sent someone to walk with me.

We have a tendency to put on a brave face in difficult circumstances, but it's scary when you feel like you need to constantly look over your shoulder.

I still vividly recall the chills that would run up my spine at the mention of this man's name. Yes, we did eventually find out his name and got a restraining order.

When a University of Nebraska at Omaha student was harassed in three separate incidents, a friend and his buddies jumped in to help.

According to the Omaha World-Herald, Shirley Rodriguez was the recipient of three very direct and very hate-filled interactions following the 2016 presidential election.

Her friend, Kain Martin, grabbed some buddies from the gym and sprung into action.

The men didn't rush into the streets looking for the perpetrators in a fit of violence.

Instead, they parked themselves at a table over the lunch hour outside the busy student center on campus.

I'm certain there had to be some funny looks. The three buff men, one with a rattlesnake tattoo on his chest, calmly sat at the table with a sign in front of them that read, "Have you felt unsafe on campus? Discriminated against? Threatened? Afraid to walk around? We will walk with you."

The men said they just wanted to get across the message that hatred would not be tolerated.

Their unique act of kindness didn't draw too many takers, but it has drawn the attention of thousands of people across the nation. Their story has gone viral.

While the heart behind their action resonated with so many people, I have to believe that the biggest impact it made was on Shirley Rodriguez herself, the 19-year-old student who had been the recipient of the hateful comments.

Instead of feeling belittled, she now knows that others are taking her hurt seriously.

When you're feeling scared, vulnerable and intimidated, having one reliable friend to walk by your side is a very good feeling.

I can only imagine what it feels like to have three large, loving men volunteering for the job.

Kindness is like a secret passageway through which God blesses us as we bless others.

Kindness Reminds Us We Have Enough

For most of my adulthood, I have mistakenly believed that kindness flows from the excess in my life.

I have extra money, I can throw a little in the jar.

I have extra time, I can offer to take a neighbor to the store.

I have extra energy, I can volunteer to read to my son's class.

Scarcity is scary. Maybe that's why the two words sound the same. It's scary to think we might not have enough if we give away what we have.

But guess what? We will never have enough. It's the great Achilles' heel of humanity: we are created to crave more.

When I started working in TV making $18,000 a year, I thought the people making $32,000 were filthy rich. When I started making $32,000 I thought, "If I only made $50,000. Then I'd finally be satisfied."

It's a vicious cycle. The more we have, the more we want. A friend once said it this way: the bigger the button, the bigger the hole. The more we cram into our shopping bags, the bigger the storage shed we'll eventually need.

This is an especially important time of year to take a good hard look at our internal thoughts on surplus and scarcity. In just a few days, we're all going to go hog wild online and in stores buying things we never knew we needed because someone tells us if we don't, we'll never get the chance again. *Hurry! Limited time only! Don't let this deal pass you up!*

Maybe we pass the deal up for ourselves, but feel like we need to buy something bigger, nicer, better for the people we love. *At this price, how can I possibly say no? It's like I'm saving money!*

I have an uneasy feeling that many of us are going to wake up mid-January and realize we are spent. Physically, emotionally and financially spent.

I'm not suggesting that we put the brakes on decorating or shopping or baking thousands of delicious cookies. I'm just suggesting that we use our limited resources on things that pay big dividends.

Like kindness. Real kindness. Not the kind of kindness that says, "I have to give them a gift because they got one for me."

Real kindness carries a risk. It forces us to trust. That's when kindness becomes beautiful and invigorating and a truly remarkable force in our lives. When we give, we get.

Kindness is like a secret passageway through which God blesses us as we bless others.

But we have to take the first step down the seemingly dark alley in order to see that we will actually be receiving much more than we're giving, when we're giving from the heart.

We are staring down the barrel of Black Friday. It's fun, it's exciting and it can also be the death of us. So this Black Friday, I'm joining a group of kindness activists to turn Black Friday into RAK Friday.

The idea is that while we go about the hustle and bustle, we spread love through Random Acts of Kindness.

Worried you don't have enough money, time or energy to make that happen? Here are a few ideas from the Random Acts of Kindness Foundation to get you started.

Smile.

Compliment a stranger in passing.

Get in touch with an old friend.

Be a positive presence on social media.

Pick up trash you see lying around.

Kindness is a simple but stunningly powerful tool to remind us that we are enough and we have enough.

For more RAK Friday ideas and encouragement to continually choose kindness, visit www.randomactsofkindness.org.

Kindness Gets the Feel-Good Chemicals Flowing

Whatever you look for is what you'll see. Don't believe me?

Think about your ex: ex-husband, ex-boyfriend, ex-wife. Since I'm a woman and I'm the one writing this, let's pick on the men for a moment. When you first met this man, the love of your life, he could do no wrong. You were drawn to each other, the chemistry was right, and everything he did was cute and quirky.

Now fast-forward.

The chemical reaction is gone, and all that's left is this guy who snores, coughs without covering his mouth and leaves his stinky socks on the floor right next to the dirty laundry hamper. *Would it be so hard to actually put them in the basket?*

When you have one foot out the door, your mind begins to look for motivation to move the other foot out the door, too.

Here's the good news: This process works in reverse, and it works on a much larger scale.

Researchers tell us that people who are kind focus more on positive social interactions. Instead of dwelling on the bad things that happen throughout the day, those who are intentionally kind begin magnifying and remembering the good.

Here's the even better news: Kindness creates serotonin, one of the body's four feel-good chemicals.

Serotonin flows when you feel significant or important. In its absence, we feel lonely and depressed. In fact, most antidepressant medication focuses on the production of serotonin.

Here's the best news: Your mind can't tell the difference between real and imaginary scenarios, so it produces serotonin when you do an act of kindness and then again when you think about the act of kindness later. It's why gratitude journals are so effective. You feel grateful and happy in the moment and then grateful and happy again when you reflect on it later in the day. Both times, your body produces serotonin as if it's actually happening for the first time.

I vividly remember my state of mind when I started writing this kindness column five years ago. I'll be honest. Life was pretty gray. I was depressed and used food, alcohol and other people's drama to create some excitement in my life. And my marriage? Well, let me just say, my poor husband. The man couldn't do anything right. My brain was trained to look for all the ways in which he failed me each day instead of all the ways he was getting it right.

One of the side effects of writing a weekly column about kindness is that I had to come up with new material every week. Sometimes readers would send in stories, just like they do now, but oftentimes I had to hunt down interesting acts of kindness. I had to look for them.

I had to be intentional, and that's when the real benefits of kindness starting taking hold in my life.

When I began to look for kindness around me, I found it. I found it at the grocery store and the airport and the bank, and most importantly, I found it in my own home.

Whether it's a newly elected politician, a difficult co-worker or a worn-out spouse, if you're looking for all the things they're doing wrong, you'll find them. Do yourself a favor and focus on what's right. The serotonin is free for the taking.

Kindness Makes Big Impact on Canadian Neighbor

Have you seen it? Have you seen the video from the marketing agency in Canada asking its citizens to tell America why it's great? I thought it had to be a sham. My normally trusting nature became skeptical. Then I watched the video. I looked into the eyes of those Canadians, and I thought, "They like us! They really like us!"

Which brings up two questions I need to ponder.

One, why does it matter?

And two, can't someone just do something nice? Does there always have to be an ulterior motive?

OK, so technically, I'm pondering three questions.

To answer the first one, "Why does it matter?," I'd say it doesn't. Just like in junior high, we don't need people to like us. We can go about our day with our nose to the ground and a chip on our shoulder and survive just fine. But what a miserable existence. It's way more fun to be surrounded by friends.

As to the second and third questions, well, I'm a little embarrassed that my initial reaction was to be cautious and distrustful of the whole "Tell America It's Great" campaign. I'm the kindness lady! I love kindness! I believe in kindness! What has happened to me? Maybe the same thing has happened to you. We're all just a little wary of anything that feels political these days.

The bottom line for me is this: If anyone anywhere thinks America is great, it's because of you.

It's because of the actions of individual people.

Individuals who build and design and fight for justice and act with kindness in their own neighborhoods are the ones who make up the cities and states and countries of which we can be proud.

It starts with just one person. Like the person who found a wallet and turned it in and made a huge impression on our north-of-the-border neighbor, Juliet, who just happened to be visiting from Canada. She was so touched that she sent me this letter, hoping to thank the anonymous do-gooder.

"On Aug. 15, a few family members and I drove down to Grand Forks for the day. When we were leaving, I was getting gas at the Holiday station on 32nd Avenue. It seems that I inadvertently put my wallet on the roof of my truck.

When we were finished getting gas, I drove back in the direction of Dollar Tree looking for a mailbox. I cut through the parking lot by Old Navy. Somewhere by the Target/Best Buy stores, the wallet must have fallen off. I didn't realize it until we got home to Winnipeg.

I was beside myself for days.

Somehow, in my heart, I thought someone who was down there from Winnipeg would find it, bring it back here and put it in our mailbox.

But I got one better!

Exactly two weeks later, we received a letter in the mail from the Grand Forks Police Department, saying that my wallet was turned in and the contents were itemized.

The money, credit cards and my citizenship card were all there.

I was ecstatic! It's at least a 15-minute drive from where it was found to the police station. The fact that someone took the time to take it to the station, in tact, makes me want to cry for joy!

Even as I'm typing this, I'm choking up.

I wish I could send that person a card or somehow let them know just how deeply I appreciate their kindness. On Sept. 9, my husband and I drove down and picked up my wallet and had a great afternoon of shopping, dinner, an overnight stay and a smooth ride home.

There's not a day that goes by that I don't think about that person. I've prayed repeatedly that God would hugely and abundantly bless them. Thank you for letting me share this with you! I'm so overwhelmed still!"

If Canadians think America is great, it's because of people who do the right thing even when no one is watching. Based on Juliet's letter and her determination to express her gratitude, I'd say Canadians are pretty great, too. Watch the Tell America it's Great video and learn more about the kindness movement at www.tellamericaitsgreat.com.

It's Not a Cellphone, It's a Vessel for Kindness

I got my first cellphone on Christmas morning, 2003. I was eight months pregnant, and if my water broke in the middle of Piggly Wiggly, my husband wanted to know about it. I thought I could just go to the customer service desk and ask them to call him, but he wasn't in favor of that plan.

I was certain this whole portable telephone thing was just a passing fad. I didn't want to waste my money knowing it would eventually fail.

Well, the cellphone fad hasn't passed quite yet, so when my 12-year-old daughter came to me asking for a phone, I did what I always do when I'm not quite sure what to do: I stalled. I told her that when she had saved up enough money for the phone of her choice, I would pay for the monthly service plan.

I figured she'd be a junior or senior in high school by the time she got the money rounded up. It's hard to come up with a lot of cash when you're a preteen without a job. Jordan, being the resourceful one, starting stashing away every bit of her allowance, gift money and cat-sitting paychecks.

A week ago, she walked into my office. "Guess what, Mom? I have enough money!"

It had been less than six months. How did that happen? Off we went to the AT&T store.

Jordan and I sat nervously across the table from the sales woman in the royal-blue shirt. I had decided to upgrade my phone since I was in need of more memory.

I was panicky about getting everything transferred from the old device to the new one.

Jordan, meanwhile, was doing everything she could not to reach over and rip open the box holding her new prized possession. I think she might have been sitting on her hands in an effort to contain herself.

I started joking about this huge rite of passage we were about to walk through.

"You're like the ear-piercer of my generation," I said to the 30-year-old woman helping us. She looked at me quizzically until I went on. "You know, we begged our moms to take us to the mall and get our ears pierced just like all of our friends? Or was that just me?"

The sales woman laughed and said, "Oh, yeah! My mom took me to Claire's Boutique, and the minute I sat in the chair and realized it was going to hurt, I changed my mind. By that time, it was too late, because I already had one ear done."

Yep. That's the rite of passage I was talking about. So glad to know I wasn't alone in that trip down memory lane.

Jordan and I left the store with two shiny new cellphones and one gently used phone (my old one) that was looking for a new home.

I called another 12-year-old I know who has also been desperately saving for a phone and made her an offer she couldn't refuse.

The next day, with my daughter and her friend standing side-by-side, I handed over my old phone.

As I did, I said just one thing: "This is not a cellphone. It is a vessel for kindness. For the past two years, this phone has never, ever been used to yell at someone, text an angry message or embarrass anyone. It doesn't know how to do that. It only knows how to be kind. Please don't teach it how to be mean. Please, keep it as a vessel of kindness."

That sweet girl looked at me wide-eyed and swore she would honor my wishes. Then my daughter added, "I'm going to make my phone a vessel for kindness, too, Mom. I like that."

If cellphones are indeed here to stay, then the only power we should give them is the power to make the world a kinder place.

Kindness Brings Joy in Times of Pain

They say when it rains, it pours. That can be true in trials, but in my life, I've found that it's also true in kindness.

In times of trouble, the smallest act of love is amplified. A note in the mail, a phone call or a text message can go far in lifting someone's spirits. I still remember the gigantic card I got when I was diagnosed with breast cancer. It was from the YMCA, and it was signed by at least a hundred people. I didn't even know most of the names, but that act of kindness hit its mark: my heart.

Don and Mary Roggenkamp of Fergus Falls, Minnesota, went through a season of trials, one right after the other. While they found lots of support from their friends and family, it was another group that touched their hearts with a special random act of kindness.

Here's their story.

"It was the day before Mother's Day 2015. On that Saturday, our lives were changed forever.

Mary hadn't been feeling well for a couple of weeks. The terrible stomach pains were too much, so a trip to the emergency room was required. After the regular tests, a CAT scan was ordered. The CAT scan showed a 4-by-7-inch tumor on one of Mary's ovaries. After hearing this, Mary said she knew it was cancer. More tests confirmed that she was right.

Lake Region Healthcare in Fergus Falls sent Mary to the University of Minnesota in Minneapolis, where she went through a nine-hour surgery and a six-day stay in the hospital. Then it was back home to Fergus Falls.

That's when the 'fun' began: chemotherapy. Those who have gone through chemo know what we mean.

As if the aches and pain from chemo, along with hair loss and feeling sick, weren't enough, Mary also became allergic to chemotherapy. Yes, this can happen.

Slowly though, the healing began. After a while, Mary was even able to go through with a total knee replacement, which she had planned on doing before the cancer surprise."

As Mary was healing, Don went in for a colonoscopy. The lab reports came back: colon cancer. This is where their story develops an interesting twist of kindness.

"Shortly after this, we received a call from our bank. Karin, at Bell Bank, asked if we could come in and meet with her. 'What's wrong?' we asked. 'Did we forget a payment? Is it something with our mortgage?'

Karin said she couldn't tell us over the phone. We needed to come see her in person.

Nervously, we headed to the bank. When we got there, Karin rounded up her troops. We had no idea that every year, Bell Bank gives their employees money for a pay-it-forward program.

These five angels, Karin, Emily, Lori, Julie and Amy, pooled their pay-it-forward money and presented us with a generous check.

It's amazing, the amount of support you get from family and friends when you go through times like this; but from a bank? We never expected that.

We want to say thank you to that army of angels and most of all, Bell Bank."

I imagine Don and Mary will look back on their cancer journeys the way I look back on mine, awestruck by the joy that can surround a time of such pain, thanks to the power of kindness.

Read about other ways Bell Bank employees are paying it forward at www.bellbanks.com/Pay-It-Forward/About.

Kindness Happens Even at the Ryder Cup

As a basketball coach's wife, there are certain away games that I've learned to watch on television. Sure, they're within driving distance, but I learned long ago to listen when my husband says "You might not like this one."

It's not that our team is going to lose. Winning or losing has nothing to do with it. What keeps me at home are the fans.

Some schools are known for harassing the opposing team's coach. That's all well and fine when the coach isn't your husband—or your father.

Several years ago, I made the mistake of brushing off Saul's warning and took two of our children to a road game. Jordan was 5, and Charlie was 3. Both were just old enough to know that people were yelling rude and intimidating things at their daddy, even if they didn't really understand what those things meant.

They're silly jabs really, wisecracks about his hair or his mom or sometimes even his wife.

Saul lets those remarks roll off his shoulders. It's all part of the game, part of the fan experience, and he uses their crazy comments as fuel to fire up his team.

My kids didn't quite see it that way and they still don't.

Honestly, I have a hard time with it, too. Some of the things they say can be downright mean.

I zip my lips and plaster a smile on my face. Or I stay home.

Sometimes I imagine what would happen if I walked over to the screaming maniac with the painted face and said, "Hey, wanna take a look at some photos of the coach when he was nursing me back to health after I had breast cancer?"

I can almost see the reaction.

I think that imaginary conversation is why I fell so in love with the Ryder Cup this year. I was captivated by one particular interaction in which a guy from Mayville, North Dakota, got caught heckling Team Europe.

Basically, here's what happened: Team Europe repeatedly missed a 12-foot putt on the eighth hole of the practice round.

David Johnson of Mayville was part of the crowd trash talking the players.

Johnson is heard yelling out, "I could make the putt," at which point the four Team Europe players invite him out on the green, slap a hundred dollar bill on the ground and tell him to prove it.

Johnson sinks it.

Here's where the kindness comes in.

All of a sudden, everybody was on the same team.

Those four players that Johnson was berating moments before began hugging him and giving him high-fives and congratulating him like longtime friends.

I'm sure they were getting annoyed at the crowd and themselves for struggling with that particular hole, but once the heckler made it, they were genuinely pleased for him.

At any point during the practice round, the members of Team Europe could have pushed back against the crowd with their own insults or dirty looks. But they didn't. They simply gave a guy a chance to prove how ridiculous his comment was.

When it turns out Johnson could actually do what he said he could do, instead of turning away with snarky comebacks about it being a lucky shot, they embraced the moment and allowed their new friend to soak in the limelight.

Kindness gives us a choice. Sometimes our kindest move is to let people's rude comments roll off our backs. But every once in awhile, kindness gives us the chance to turn frustration into a fairy tale ending.

Layers of Kindness Make a Difference in the Life of a Man with Down Syndrome

As I opened my email, I really thought the sender was about to share a story of cookie-making kindness. It was early in the morning, and my first pre-coffee thought was, "Oh, how sweet of them."

Then I kept reading.

Then I read it again.

Then I wrote back and asked her to tell me more—more about her son, his work and his story.

I could see layer upon layer of kindness, and all of a sudden, I was inspired by a man I had never met.

Teri Johnson sent me this story about her son. I wonder if you can see the layers of kindness, too?

"As I helped my son, Blake, prepare treats for his co-workers to celebrate his one-year anniversary at his job, I realized I had to share this story of kindness. It was his idea to bring sports cookies to the guys at work to say thank you.

Blake is our first born and will turn 23 years old Oct. 28. It is ironic that he was born in October, which we found out much later, is Down Syndrome awareness month. As the saying goes, 'Down Syndrome is a journey I never planned, but I sure do love my tour guide!'

Blake graduated with his brother, Alec, from Fargo North High School in 2013.

Much to Blake's delight, he was able to stay at North two more years for some 'post-grad' work while his brother headed to college.

As he neared the end of his time at North, people would ask Blake what he was going to do after high school. He'd always respond, 'I'm going to work at Buffalo Wild Wings.' We apparently had visited the restaurant more times than I'd like to admit.

My husband, Steve, and I wrestled with making plans for the next phase of Blake's life. What would we find to make him feel productive and challenged?

My husband approached the Buffalo Wild Wings manager with an idea: Could Blake work there if we provided a job coach?

Prior to the interview, we had done some role playing to prepare him for questions we thought the manager, Jeremy, may ask. Blake was ready!

Jeremy said that when he was wrapping up the interview, he asked Blake if he had any questions for him. (Oops! We hadn't anticipated that.) The manager said Blake paused, looked down at his folded hands, then looked him straight in the eye and stated, 'I love work.' Jeremy hired him on the spot.

We knew our prayers had been answered when we saw Blake's reaction to an upcoming family trip.

We were lucky enough to be headed to Tampa, Florida for the Frozen Four in April 2016.

Blake watched his favorite team, the University of North Dakota, win its eighth Division I Men's Hockey National Championship. He even got a piece of the net!

We were shocked when he didn't seem as excited to go as we thought he would've been. When we asked what the problem was, he responded, 'I have to work.' He looked at us very seriously and said, 'They need me.'

In those three words, it was clear how his co-workers made Blake feel: needed, respected and more alike than different. They may not realize that the kindness they show him in the kitchen makes such an impact."

Can you see the layers of kindness? An employee who brings cookies, a brother who walked through high school with his best friend, a mom and dad concerned for their son's future, a manager who gives a guy a chance, and co-workers who welcome him into the fold. It illustrates the truth that wherever you are and whatever you do, kindness matters. It always makes a difference.

Using Kindness to Make up for Lost Time

I'm a sucker for a romantic story. I'll tell anyone who will listen that I fell in love with my husband when I was in sixth grade. True, he wouldn't date me until I was 24, but that just adds to the charm. Ever seen *50 First Dates* or *Message in a Bottle*? How about *Sleepless in Seattle* or *You've Got Mail*? I've seen them all and I have half of them memorized.

I love a good romance. I think you get my point.

I felt like I got my own message in a bottle when I received a letter from Fargo, North Dakota resident Jim Field. He is making up for lost time and he's using kindness to woo the woman he says he never should have lost in the first place.

Here's his story:

"After moving to Fargo last year, I became reunited with a gal I used to date right after I got out of the United States Marine Corps in the early 1970s. Her husband of 40 years had just passed away and we met at the wake.

We started out simply by reminiscing. For six months we shared phone calls, coffee and lunch dates. Finally, I asked her out for dinner. When she came over to my place to pick me up, she came in the door and I said, 'Stop. Hold it.' She looked at me somewhat bewildered. 'Bonnie, you are a very attractive woman,' I continued. 'You look really nice!'

She did look lovely in the new clothes she bought just for this dinner date. I was wearing a new suit I bought at Macy's for the occasion.

The look in her beautiful green eyes, along with her words, told me 'Thank you.' I could tell she was thirsty to hear something nice.

Compliments can pay dividends! We went out to dinner at the Mezzaluna restaurant on Roberts Street and we are now together again after all these years.

We have a lot of catching up to do. I'm showering her with TLC like it's going out of style: flowers, candy and ice cream, too!

People need to hear something nice and you just don't know what that comment will do. Destiny? Possibly. Fate? Who knows. I should have never let that one go so many years ago."

Jim's story could have been peeled straight from a Nicholas Sparks' script. He and Bonnie are planning a trip to Italy and they intend to visit lots of other lovely places in the near future. Jim says he feels like he has a new lease on life.

He also says hindsight is 20/20. And he's right. But the good news is, it's never too late for love and it's never too late for kindness. We never have to wonder if we've done the right thing or taken the right fork in the road if we are being kind along the way. Eventually, life will lead us back to where we're supposed to be.

If we're lucky, there's a hand to hold when we get there and plenty of years to continue using kindness to make up for lost time.

When we are
treated well, let
it serve as a
reminder to
treat others
well.

Don't Let Appearances Get in the Way of Kindness

Most of the time when I go to Walmart I am showered and wearing real clothes. I say most of the time, because I have been known to make a quick run for supplies in my pajamas.

My most recent trip to the store included me, not only showered, but also wearing mascara, lipstick, black pants and a stylish blue shirt. A purse on my arm and designer sunglasses on my head, I grabbed a cart and smiled at the greeter.

Thirty minutes later, I was on my way out loaded down with bags of merchandise.

Also in the cart were four cardboard boxes containing a slew of spiral bound notebooks. I was working on a project and needed to buy the notebooks by the case.

The greeter stopped me. "Excuse me, ma'am. May I please see your receipt?"

For the teeny-tiniest second, I wanted to roll my eyes. The notebooks were 17 cents a piece. Why would I steal four cases of notebooks?

The woman took a quick look at the receipt, then a quick look at the cart and sent me on my way.

I was inconvenienced by about 7 seconds.

As I headed out the automatic doors, I heard the greeter ask the man behind me if she could see his receipt.

Pushing the cart out to my car, it dawned on me. Why wouldn't she ask to see my receipt? Because I look like I can afford to pay? Since when does looking tired, haggard or dirty mean that you are a shoplifter? Can't people in nice clothes steal, too?

Then I realized a truth about myself that hurt. I am outwardly kind to people, but somewhere in the deepest recesses of my heart, I am unkind. I automatically judge others with a measuring stick I would never want used on myself or any of the people I love.

Most of the time, most of the places I go, I am treated with favor. I am waited on quickly and courteously. Sometimes the manager of the grocery store will even open a new checkout lane when I'm standing in line. I suspect it's because he knows I'm the basketball coach's wife.

Does that happen to the beaten-down mom with three kids in tow who will be paying with food stamps? I hope so, but I don't know.

I asked a group of friends from various parts of the country if they felt like they were treated better when they dressed nicely. Out of more than 50 people, only five said that they didn't think clothing or grooming made a difference. The rest of the group weighed in with an emphatic "Yes" and went on to give specific examples at stores, airports, car dealerships and doctors' offices.

Could it be possible that we treat others better when we feel better about ourselves? Do we feel better about ourselves when we're more put together? Do looks really make a difference? These questions have intrigued researchers for decades.

What I know is this: to whom much is given, much is expected. I have an obligation to love others well, lavishly even, in whatever capacity I can. Sometimes that means giving my time, talent or resources. And sometimes it means inviting that weary mom to go ahead of me in the newly opened checkout lane.

When we are treated well, let it serve as a reminder to treat others well. Regardless of how they look, how they speak, or whether or not they're still in their pajamas.

Kindness Makes the Best First Day Ever

Some of the most amazing teachers don't ever get to stand up in front of the class. They don't get to use the staff lounge or open gifts of appreciation at the end of the year. They are teachers who masquerade as students who have special needs.

Dawn Bolstad is passionate about working with students who, she says, teach without saying a word.

"When they reach for your hand, it is because they see you for who you are. When they love you, it is without pretense. When they celebrate, it is without restraint.

Working with these kids is, without question, the most amazing gift of acceptance one human being can give another."

The first day of classes at Fargo North High School looked a little different than normal thanks to an act of kindness by Bolstad's students, plus three more young people from Rene'e Schwandt's classroom.

Just before the first day of school, Bolstad took a tiny idea and put it into action. She brought it up to the administration, who gave an enthusiastic green light. Then she mentioned it to the music teacher, who put together a rockin' playlist. Thanks to a conversation with her teaching team, she found two middle school girls who were willing to put their artistic talents to work.

Finally, it was time to add the most important element. Her students.

One by one, as the Fargo North students walked up to the school for the first day of class, they were greeted by a very exuberant cheering section.

Signs lined the walkway with messages proclaiming "This is your moment," "Be your best self," "You are unique" and "We are North."

Eleven students, who are usually working in the classroom on life skills, showed off the most important life skill of all: kindness. They waved pom-pons, wore fun hats and danced to inspiring songs like "Brave" and "Eye of the Tiger."

Bolstad says the effect was breath-taking.

"The teens were walking up to the school looking sad and frustrated. But after seeing my students and hearing people yell 'Happy first day of school!' 'I'm so glad you're here!' and 'You look great!' those furrowed brows turned to smiles. The kids even stood up straighter."

Out of hundreds of students, there were only three who didn't smile or want to walk through the fanfare.

Bolstad says she knows who they are and is determined to find them and make sure they know they are loved and appreciated at their school.

"Imagine walking into the first day of school greeted by people who have no other agenda than to wish you well. That's an experience that cannot be distilled into a number, a value. That's an experience all of us deserve.

It is so unbelievably cool that kids with more challenges than any of us can really imagine are encouraging their classmates.

Dawn Bolstad has been teaching for 29 years. That's 29 first days of school, but she says thanks to kindness, this one was her all-time favorite.

Kindness Eases Growing Pains

My little girl's shoulders slumped as she got in the minivan.

"The whole team was invited, Mom. I was the only one not included."

Seventh grade is hard. I know, I did it once. I'd go from elation to desperation and back again in five minutes flat. My poor parents.

Later that night, with Jordan's wounds fresh on my heart, I was scrolling through Facebook when a friend's post caught my attention:

"My heart is breaking. It happened. My biggest fear when it comes to letting my baby girl go to kindergarten. I could tell something was not right when I picked her up from school. She came home, went to her room and shut the door. I stood outside her door and asked if she was OK. She swung her door opened, practically knocked me over with a hug and started bawling. She said the girl who lives across the street would not be her friend. She and another girl were teasing my daughter at recess and no one would play with her. It's already starting."

Another momma, many states away, with a daughter just starting school, was grieving for her baby the way I was grieving for mine. But we weren't the only ones.

What struck me most about that post was the amount of responses from people. Women in all different phases of motherhood sharing their hearts, saying "I've been there."

We've all been there, either as parents or in our own childhood. My husband says it's a rite of passage. As long as time has existed, kids have had to learn social behavior from the school of hard knocks.

Yes, but ...

Couldn't we give them some tools to make it a touch more bearable? Couldn't we teach them that we all feel better when we lead with kindness?

Is there a solution? I don't know. I want to say yes. I want to say it has something to do with kindness, but specifically, what kind of kindness?

My eyes turned again to the comments left by other moms. This time, instead of just noticing the unity, I saw ideas of ways to nurture our children and ourselves pouring from the page.

"Find out if she can pair up with a buddy."

"Empower her to look for someone else who needs a friend."

"Talk to the teacher."

"At Nativity they have kids that volunteer to be 'Peace Keepers' during recess. Their job is to look for kids who aren't playing with others or are being picked on and go to them. Maybe you could suggest that concept to your principal?"

"Maybe having her pray for the other girls would be a good idea."

"Walk across the street and talk to the mom and daughter. Suggest they start over and become friends."

"Tell her to put herself out there and say hi to someone she doesn't know!"

"I always took the angle that little kids that act that way probably have very unhappy lives. I told my kids that maybe someone has been very mean to that little girl and that's why she is mean."

"Does the school have a friend bench? I've heard about them: just sit on the bench and then other kids will know you're looking for a friend to play with."

"The 'Daniel Tiger' television series is based on Mr. Rogers and is great for empathy and emotional skills."

"Good snuggles and a good night sleep sometimes do the trick. Monday is a new day with new friends to be made."

All of our children are going to experience growing pains as they work their way through childhood. We all did. I'm sharing these ideas in the hopes that a combination of any of the above, along with a strong dose of love from mom and dad, will help make the journey a little more pleasant.

Why I Agree to Be Uncomfortable for Kindness

Why do I do this to myself? I could have said no. Why didn't I say no? They're going to eat me alive!

My introverted self is verbally attacking the ambitious dynamo part of my personality. You see, go-getter me signed up for something that is now making me a little sick to my stomach.

I often feel like I am two people in one body. I'm a huge cheerleader for kindness. I will put myself out there any day of the week to persuade people that kindness can change a life. It's changed my life. That's why I'm so passionate. But deep down I'm an introverted, need-my-space, let's just all quietly go about our business person.

That's the side of my brain that's freaking out right now.

Why? I'm so glad you asked.

I have agreed to talk to several hundred kids, kindergarten through sixth grade, at an all-school morning meeting. Twenty minutes, me with a microphone, and a bunch of kids who want to be at recess. What could possibly go wrong?

As I was pondering the idea of moving to a remote island, I stumbled across a few emails. They were from teachers who were sharing the development of character that happens when kids learn about kindness.

Here's the first one. A friend of mine sent this about a high school student named Kate:

"Check this out! Kate's advice to new high schoolers at orientation today was a call for kindness. 'Be nice to people,' she said. Her comment, 'It's nice to be important, but it's more important to be nice' got a round of applause from the audience. What a great kid!"

Then I saw this email from a teacher named Becky Fisher:

"I wanted to share my experience with kindness. I have the privilege of working with Fargo middle school students. This past spring, my classes discussed Ron Clark's 'Essential 55' rules. Rule No. 11 is about acts of kindness. These acts are not just simply picking up something that was dropped or holding open a door, but rather deliberate, thought-out acts, complete with an executable plan.

After our discussion, I challenged my students to perform an act of kindness. One month later, I asked them to write about their experience.

I was blown away at the depth of their commitment to being kind. Students cleaned the house and watched younger siblings. One boy put together an entertainment stand for his mother, while others cooked dinner for their family with dessert. Another student volunteered her time at a resale store and straightened shelves to make it easier for the shoppers.

One girl, whose family had benefitted from the community's help in the past, found someone going through similar circumstances. She created a silent auction item, then asked her mother to drive her to deliver it. The two of them were able to spend time with this hurting family and encourage them.

These students came up with some thoughtful acts of kindness. I could not be more proud."

I'm so glad these teachers took the time to share the impact of kindness on kids' lives, because it changed my perspective.

I'm no longer fearful of losing control of an auditorium full of students. Instead, I will put on my cutest outfit, load up a bagful of props and march right on over to that school.

Because kindness matters.

If we won't step out of our comfort zone and teach kids how much fun it is to be radically kind, who will? How will they ever learn?

So, I'm sorry, Introverted Self. This time, the kindness-loving go-getter wins out.

To read all of Ron Clark's "Essential 55" rules, visit ronclarkacademy.com.

The Power of One Kind Word

We were wrong. As children we stuck our tongues out at the playground bully and hollered with a fake bravado, "Sticks and stones may break my bones but words will never hurt me." We were wrong.

Wikipedia tells me this childhood rhyme has been around since 1862. For 150 years we have been telling ourselves that words don't matter. But they do.

A year after having my third baby, a man at the gym said to me, "With as much as you work out, I'd think you'd be thin by now." I laughed good-naturedly and made a comment about my love for chocolate, but I walked away wounded.

Mean words hurt. They stick.

But kind words stick, too.

I remember the boy in elementary school who spoke up in music class the day I was too scared to try out for the musical. I wanted the part of Dorothy, but I was too shy to actually sing about any rainbows. In front of 20 third-grade classmates, Dean Zavadsky bravely stood up and said, "It's OK, Nicki. Just sing it. We promise not to laugh at you."

I sang the song and I got the part. Many years later I would represent the state of Wisconsin by singing on stage at the Miss America Pageant. I wonder if Dean even remembers the way he breathed encouragement into a young girl's heart that day? Nearly 35 years later, I remember.

I've been the recipient of many words of encouragement throughout the years. I assume everyone has a circle of personal cheerleaders, but maybe not.

I got a message from a woman who goes to my church. I don't actually know her very well. I have only spoken to her one time in passing.

She told me I could share her note with you in hopes of illustrating the impact of one kind word.

"Hi Nicole, I have wanted to tell you something for a long time. The day you and your husband were confirmed into our church, you gave me a compliment. You simply said, 'That color looks beautiful on you.' Please don't think I'm a whiner, but rarely do I receive compliments about my looks, particularly from a stranger. I think I might have given you an odd look because I thought 'Why is this stranger being nice?' I guess I was suspicious because people who are that nice to me usually want something. At least that's what I used to think.

As time passed I learned what a truly genuine person of faith and kindness you are. Therefore, I began to feel bad about the look I gave you.

My husband and I have welcomed our first grandchild into the world and I have retired from my business to pursue other interests, both professional and personal.

You have impacted me more than you will ever know. Your one sentence of kindness has truly changed my life."

Can you imagine the rush of love I felt when reading this letter?

We all have times, like I did standing in the church that day. A lovely thought flickers into our minds, *That woman looks so beautiful in that color.*

Do we keep it to ourselves, wasting an easy opportunity to brighten someone's day or do we give it away freely?

Sticks and stones may break our bones, but the power of words is also in our control. Will your words be the gift that quenches a thirsty soul or the dagger that hits an already hurting heart?

Kindness Found in Bathrooms and Backseats

There are certain conversations I'm sure God never intended us to have with each other. Like in high school, when my poor dad seemed to pale a little every time I asked him for money for bras or tampons. That's just not a comfortable conversation.

Single dads are raising daughters, and single moms are stepping up to coach their sons' baseball teams. I'm not saying it's wrong or that we're not equipped because of gender, I'm just saying the lines get a little blurry when we hold them up to past standards like June and Ward Cleaver.

The world we live in is confusing, isn't it?

You know where it gets really messy? The bathroom.

I write about kindness, so I'm not going to weigh in on any transgender bathroom issues. That's not where I'm going. Instead, I'm talking about kids who need to use the bathroom and the parents who have to wait outside.

Traveling alone with my sons is terrifying. I stand anxiously outside busy men's airport bathrooms praying there is only one exit.

On more than one occasion, when things have been taking a little longer than normal, my mama bear instincts have kicked in. Yes, I've been that woman, closing my eyes and stepping just one toe into the men's room so I could holler at my kids. Relief like none other fills my heart as I hear their voices and my panic recedes.

I've been on the other end of that situation more times than I can count.

I step out of the ladies' room and straight into the path of a fidgety father, who sheepishly asks if I would go back in and check on his daughter.

I know the feeling, so I'm always happy to help.

Carolyn Erickson from Amidon, North Dakota, sent me a letter about her own bathroom kindness. Sure, she wasn't dealing with a child, but she did step up with a solution when it mattered most for the person in front of her.

"I was eating at Applebee's in Dickinson when I excused myself to use the bathroom. I noticed the cleaning crew was working in the men's room with the door propped open. As I was leaving the ladies' room, a young man, perhaps in his 20s, realized he was unable to get into the men's restroom.

I told him, 'There are no women in the ladies' room. Why don't you let Grandma guard the door while you use it?'

When he came out, looking much relieved with a big smile on his face, he said, 'I love you, Grandma!'

I made his day, and he made mine!"

Carolyn's kindness isn't reserved for the restroom.

She also mentioned in her letter that she and her husband feel an "empty back seat in our vehicle doesn't make much sense," so they offer rides to people who need to make a trip to the bank, pharmacy or grocery store.

What a great way to get to know people. I bet having new friends in the car opens the door for a lot of conversations that God is not only happy we're having, but actually divinely appointed.

Rummage Sale Cash and Kindness Come in Handy

Red and blue lights whirled in my rearview mirror. Uh oh. Someone was in big trouble. I turned the corner and drove another block before the police car came up behind me. I pulled over to allow the officer room to pass. After all, I am a law-abiding citizen.

Imagine my surprise when the officer pulled over right behind me.

Imagine my double surprise when I realized I was being pulled over right in front of my husband's office.

Imagine my triple surprise when I saw my husband walk out of the building at that exact moment.

I was mortified.

My husband has called me "Gordon Leadfoot" for years. I think it's a compliment because he has such a great respect for the singer/songwriter Gordon Lightfoot, but maybe not.

Perhaps he just enjoys a clever play on words and making fun of his wife.

Anyway, I knew I would never live this down.

Saul walked up to the officer and cheerfully exclaimed, "Thank you, sir, for keeping our streets safe! It's important that hoodlums, like this woman, know they can't get away with breaking the law."

The confused policeman watched as my husband handed me $20 and told me to keep the change.

I had been speeding, but thanks to North Dakota law, my ticket came to a whopping $10.

Yes, dear people who live in every other state in America, North Dakotans are so nice even their speeding tickets feel like a gift. Unless your husband is standing there watching. Then you just want to crawl under the seat and let your 10-year-old take the wheel.

I explained to both the officer and my husband that I was so busy singing with my children, who were in the backseat, that I hadn't realized the decline in the speed limit.

Neither man seemed super impressed with my parenting.

Luckily, I know other people can relate to my story. We've all been there in one way or another, feeling the tinge of red in our cheeks as an embarrassing moment comes upon us.

Judy Bristol from Fargo, North Dakota shared her own story with me.

"Last summer I was going to the clinic for an appointment. I didn't miss my billfold until I went to pay for my lunch. I had my emergency rummage sale cash in my car, so I went and got that.

About that time, my husband called and asked what I was doing. When I told him I was out for lunch, he wanted to know how I had paid for it.

It turns out my billfold wasn't just left at home, it had truly been lost. A woman had found it near a busy stop light four blocks from our house! She called my home phone and told my husband she had it. He had already gone and picked it up for me.

A couple of weeks later, I finally got to her house with a gift certificate to thank her in person. Her husband didn't even know she had done this great act of kindness! What a 'Fargo nice' lady she is!"

Thanks Judy! I think we can learn another lesson from you today: always keep a stash of rummage sale cash handy—for misplaced billfolds or speeding tickets.

Grab Kindness Before it Flies By

I was trying to fly home from New York earlier this month. I say "trying" because it was evident that it was going to take some effort.

A big storm had swept through the day before and grounded most of the planes flying out of JFK airport. So there I was at Gate C4, just me, my 12-year-old daughter and a few hundred of the angriest people you have ever met.

I can understand where their irritability had come from. After switching gates twice and then waiting through two delays, I wasn't exactly thrilled to be sitting in a sticky plastic chair with an oversized carry-on bag on my lap.

Airports are great for people watching and eavesdropping, so I began to listen in on the cellphone conversations taking place around me. "I cannot stand this!" "I'm never flying this airline again." "I haven't slept in 22 hours." "I might as well walk home at this point."

As the delays dragged on, people became more resentful of their lost time.

The problem is, they didn't quite know where to lay the blame, so they took it out on the person standing in front of them. Her name was Maria. I know that because I looked at her name tag.

Maria's shift started right after the second delay was announced. She had been off for the previous two days and had no idea that her assigned gate would look like a Times Square riot. The volume of the hornet's nest began to rise the minute the travelers saw her.

I sat in shock as I watched people call her nasty names, insist to talk to a nonexistent manager, and practically crawl over the counter to get a better look at her computer screen.

To appease those who had been re-booked on my flight, Maria called for volunteers who would be willing to hitch a later ride. She was offering $400 a seat.

My daughter and I looked at each other and my hand shot up in the air. "We'll take them."

"OK, thank you," Maria hurriedly replied. "Just wait over there and I'll get back to you once we get this plane loaded."

Jordan and I sat off to the side and continued to watch people verbally abuse this poor worker. Eventually though, the mob disappeared down the ramp and all was quiet.

When Maria came over to us, we asked her if we could perhaps take a flight the next day so that we could spend one more night in New York City.

"Sure, but I'm afraid we can't pay for a hotel or meals. All I can give you are two $400 flight vouchers."

"That's OK," I said. And then, just before she turned away, I felt compelled to say something else. "Maria, I'm so sorry for the way people have treated you today. I can tell by your demeanor that you are a lovely person. I just wanted you to know that."

Maria paused. The look in her eyes told me that she was touched by my simple and true words. She exhaled, smiled and then said, "Thank you."

When she returned a few minutes later, she handed me two vouchers for $500 each, $100 more than we had been promised.

She also had two private shuttle vouchers in her hand so we could get downtown and back for free—another savings of $100.

I didn't say nice words to Maria to get something in return. I just saw an injustice and did the only thing I could do in that moment. But that's what kindness is about. We can't control the negativity of the world around us, but we can add our own unique light and make it a more positive place for the person standing in front of us.

Nurses Fill a Painful Road with Kindness

"This needs sugar!" a woman barks from the table behind me. A nurse gently tells her for the 10th time, "I already put sugar on it for you, Alice." "Well it doesn't taste like it!" her surly charge growls.

"Help! Help! Help!" the woman two tables away shrieks. The first time I heard it, I was shocked when no one jumped up and ran frantically to her aid. Eventually I realized it's the only word she ever says. Walking the halls later in the day, I can still hear her yelling, "Help! Help! Help!"

Then there is the woman who eats her lunch while chanting, "I want to die and I don't know why." She says it almost as one would recite a childhood nursery rhyme. It would be funny if it weren't so sad.

My dad shouldn't be here. Two months ago he was flying to South Carolina for a family vacation with my sister. In my eyes, he is strong, healthy, able. He is not old in the way these people are old.

My dad was playing cards on a beautiful summer afternoon when his hand went numb. His friends called the ambulance. Stroke.

Now my father is weak, thin and unable to form cohesive thoughts, use the bathroom, or even sit up by himself.

I've been sitting by his side for a week, soaking in the cadence of this new life; the beeping of an alarm every time a nurse is called, which happens at least every three minutes.

When do they ever sit down?

I know I will forever remember the smell of disinfectant that becomes a welcome aroma as it masks the other odors that happen when one can't control one's bodily functions.

I hold my dad's hand and brush his hair and kiss the part of his face that still has feeling. It's a blessing to be here. I thank God, not for the pain we are going through (I'm not there yet), but for the joy that exists alongside it. I get to be with my dad. I get to tell him I love him and that he is a good man.

After a week, I have to go home. I'm a mom and a wife and my little tribe needs me.

It's heartbreaking, wanting to be in two places at once. But there is something else I've noticed while sitting in this rehab facility/nursing home: this place is filled with kindness. It is filled with people who have been created to help. They change stinky bed pans and cook warm meals and cover medicine in applesauce to coax it down a dry throat.

My dad and the other residents are in a vulnerable spot. They have to rely on the staff to tend to their every need. It's stressful for the patients and the nurses. It has to be. I've never once seen a nurse sitting down.

But I have seen them laughing with the residents and listening patiently to their concerns and smiling cheerfully as they greet each one by name. This isn't just a job for them, this is a calling on their lives.

Suzanne, the CNA, just brought my sleeping dad a glass of fresh water.

She readjusts the blanket around his feet and whispers to me, "I just hate it when my toes are tucked in too tightly."

Then she winks and walks away.

It's the little things that resonate the loudest when there's not much else that can be done.

My dad is so far away in so many ways, but he's coming around. And I'm grateful to know that until that happens, he will be surrounded by people who are filling the road with kindness.

Kindness & Gas Money Rescue the Empty

When the world is closing in on you, and panic and uncertainty threaten to swallow you whole, kindness takes on a new level of importance. An otherwise small gesture of love becomes magnified and gives us the strength to put one foot in front of the other.

Zach Wilson sent me this letter from a friend who found kindness at the end of the rope.

"I was driving to pick up a graduate student from China at a local airport, and all the while I thought I might be dying. It was ironic, because I had never smoked and had lived a healthy life, but I was going to be tested for lung cancer that afternoon. After years of chest pain, I was worried. Ironic things can still kill you. The chances of survival from lung cancer are not good, and I had a family to take care of.

So I was quite distracted, and not my usual self, when I realized my car was running out of gas. And then the second awareness hit: I had no money. I might be late to pick up the graduate student, after planning the trip for months, because I had no money. No cash, no debit card, no credit card, no checks.

Figuring that I might be able to at least use the number of my debit card to access my bank account, I went into a gas station. No luck. I tried a clerk in a bank, inside a nearby supermarket. Nothing doing. I asked the bank manager. He, too, said there was no way to make it happen. But, just when I was about to ask where the nearest branch of my bank was, he opened his wallet and asked me how much money I needed.

I told the man that I thought $5 would get me to the airport. As he handed it to me, I was overcome with emotion. I blurted out my thanks with a half-sob, and left, only to find that I couldn't figure out where I had parked the car. Glancing around, I saw the manager had followed me out of the store, and was looking at me with concern.

Sometimes, thoughts just flit through your mind. For a second, I wondered if he was going to call the police because I was acting so strangely. I had a sense of urgency about not wandering around. So I pulled myself together long enough to find my car and climb inside. The manager, apparently satisfied that I was safe, went back in the store.

I remember being so relieved when I got into the car. But, at the same time, I was thinking, 'You still have to get to the airport.'

I started driving again. At some point, I realized $5 would get me there, but it wasn't going to bring me back. Whatever. I would have to deal with that when I got there.

I arrived on time in spite of everything, and asked the visiting student, a little embarrassed, if she had any American money. Luckily, she did, and I borrowed a few dollars to buy gas for the rest of the trip.

That evening I got a call with the results from the CT scan. I did not have lung cancer! Good news, but the bad news was that they still didn't know what was going on with my lungs.

I stayed busy with my kids, work and medical tests. There was plenty to do. Many weeks later, the doctors discovered that I had a very rare form of a different kind of cancer.

Five and a half rounds of chemo and six difficult months later, the cancer is gone; the graduate student returned to China after an internship in the states; and I anonymously sent the bank manager $20 in return for his trouble. I hope he knows how much his kindness meant to me.

That whole time was a difficult one, but it taught me to appreciate whatever kindness I can find, to keep going, and try to remember where I parked my car."

One senseless, over-the-top act of kindness is all it takes to remind me that I'm still good, and so are most people.

Courageous Kindness Combats Selfishness

The bad thing about striving to live a life of kindness is that you realize when you fail. And you fail every day. Or maybe I should say, *I fail every day.*

The minute I keep the conversation trivial to avoid entering someone's pain, the minute I cut the conversation short with an impatient answer, the minute I lower my eyes to the ground to avoid being asked for help, I feel my failure.

It wasn't always like that. I used to be able to brush off my haughtiness like I would brush lint off a black T-shirt. Something has changed along the way. My blind spots are becoming more narrow and I'm able to see when my actions are not led by love.

The failures happen every day. Yet, each day I'm also spurred to continue striving toward kindness because it feels so good when I get it right. Like I'm powerful and whole and somehow healthier.

In his commencement address to the 2013 graduates of Syracuse University, writer and professor George Saunders philosophically diagnosed a sickness in each one of us. It's called selfishness.

That's it. When selfishness wins, I feel sick. Sick in my mind, sick in my soul, sometimes even sick to my stomach.

My friend recently reminded me of Saunders' profound words when she sent me a quote she ran across from that same commencement speech.

Saunders said, "What I regret most in my life are failures of kindness. Those moments when another human being was there, in front of me, suffering, and I responded ... sensibly. Reservedly. Mildly."

Being sensibly kind won't change your life. It won't get you to the place where joy lives.

You need to stretch, reach a little further and get uncomfortable.

You need to be willing to get hurt or even risk hurting another as you step into their pain on the way to healing.

That happens when we make eye contact, refuse to stay superficial and step over the boundaries that society has set by being courageously kind.

It doesn't happen overnight, but it does happen.

I can look back over the past 40 years and pinpoint when I found true happiness. It was the same time I started writing about kindness and working diligently to be intentionally kind.

Selfishness is real and it threatens to overtake me daily, but on those days, one senseless, over-the-top act of kindness is all it takes to remind me that I'm still good, and so are most people. Kindness is like medicine. Take two a day and call me in the morning.

I'm not saying you can't ever let the phone go to voicemail when you know it's a needy neighbor or spend the extra five bucks in your wallet on yourself. I'm just suggesting that you make kindness your go-to plan most of the time.

Or as Saunders so fittingly put it, "Do all the other things, the ambitious things — travel, get rich, get famous, innovate, lead, fall in love, make and lose fortunes, swim naked in wild jungle rivers (after first having it tested for monkey poop) — but as you do, to the extent that you can, *err in the direction of kindness.*"

Airmen Bond Through Kindness of Kidney Donation

Life can change in an instant. One moment you're young and in love and planning a wedding, and the next, you're sitting in a hospital room trying to decipher medical jargon and test results.

That's how it went for Aly Cola. In a matter of days, her life was turned upside down. Thanks to a great act of kindness, it has been put right-side up once again.

Here's her story:

"My husband, Daniel Cola, is a staff sergeant in the United States Air Force, as well as an NYPD officer. He is the epitome of service and humility and has known that he wanted to serve both our country and community since he was a kid. We are high school sweethearts. He is the love of my life, my best friend, my other half, my partner and the best person I know.

However, our marriage did not get off to the easiest start.

My husband had contracted Dengue Fever, which is a mosquito-borne disease that lowered his kidney function to less than 20 percent. When he still hadn't recovered after two weeks in the hospital, doctors did a biopsy, which unmasked Daniel's chronic kidney disease.

As crazy as it sounds, the Dengue Fever was a blessing in disguise, because otherwise we would have never known anything was wrong with his kidneys! Apparently, you can remain quite well until late in chronic renal failure.

Daniel's doctors eventually referred us to a transplant team. I was not a match for Daniel, but I was cleared to be a donor, so we decided to participate in a kidney swap with other potential donors and recipients.

We were on the kidney swap list for about two months when my husband received a text from an Air Force co-worker, Master Sergeant Henry Windels.

Though Henry and my husband work in different sections of Stuart Air Force Base in Newburgh, N.Y., they have been friendly for the past few years.

Henry noticed that he hadn't seen Daniel in a while. A co-worker told Henry everything that had happened. A few days later Henry contacted Daniel via text and said, 'I am sorry to hear about your troubles, my family and I are praying for you. I have wanted to donate my kidney for a long time, I have especially wanted to donate it to a veteran. I will not take no for an answer, I want to donate my kidney to you. Please tell me how I sign up to get tested.' We couldn't believe it!

Getting cleared to be a donor is no easy task. Henry participated in loads of blood tests, MRIs, ultrasounds, EKGs and urine analysis tests. Henry was a match and the transplant took place on Oct. 6, 2015.

Henry is very literally saving Daniel's life. Thanks to Henry, I do not have to start planning my husband's funeral. Thanks to Henry, I can enjoy many more anniversaries with my husband. Thanks to Henry, my husband will be able to return to work, eat and exercise like he used to. What Henry is doing truly demonstrates the highest degree of brotherhood and humility. There are no words for his kindness."

Removing the Black Dot Makes Room for Kindness

One day, a professor presented his pupils with a pop quiz. As the students filed into the classroom, they saw a piece of paper on each desk, face down.

When everyone was seated, the professor told them to turn over the papers. To everyone's surprise, there were no questions, just a black dot in the center of the sheet. The professor, seeing the confusion on the students' faces, simply said, "Write about what you see."

Toward the end of class, the professor collected all the exams and started reading each one out loud, in front of the students.

All of them, with no exception, defined the black dot, trying to explain its position in the center of the sheet.

When he had finished reading them all, the professor said, "I'm not going to grade you on this, I just wanted to give you something to think about. No one wrote about the white part of the paper. Everyone focused on the black dot. The same happens in our lives. We have a white piece of paper to observe and enjoy, but we always focus on the dark spots: the health issues, the lack of money, the complicated relationships. The dark spots are very small when compared to everything else in our lives, but they're the ones that pollute our minds. Our life is a gift given to us by God. There are always reasons to celebrate. Change your focus. Learn to see the white space on the page instead of the black dot."

My friend, Galo Kostka, sent me that short story in an email.

I'm not sure who originally wrote it, but I took the liberty of modifying it a bit for this column.

When I first read it, I thought about all of the daily things that threaten to steal my joy.

The little black dots, like sticky countertops and messy rooms, can quickly become magnified and eclipse the blessings of actually having countertops or things to put in those rooms.

The second time I read it, I thought about my job as a parent.

Would my children look back and see my blunders, my black dots, or would they see their childhood as a mostly clean, bright, white piece of paper?

The third time I read it, I thought about my own childhood.

I look back far too often and remember the divorce, the times my dad was too strict or not strict enough, and the times I was left to figure things out on my own. I forget about all the white spaces.

Dad, in honor of Father's Day, I'm stealing this little section of the paper to tell you that I remember the good stuff. I hope you know I do.

I remember being 6 years old and singing "Home, Home on the Range" at the top of our lungs as we rode horseback all over the countryside.

I remember being 14 and stepping on your toes as some poor cowboy tried to teach us the two-step, and being secretly proud to dance with my dad.

I remember being 16 and nursing a heartache and you cutting a quote from the newspaper for me that said, "Instead of waiting for someone to bring you flowers, go plant your own garden."

You always believed in me, Dad, when I wanted to be a model or live in France or become Miss Wisconsin. You never once doubted I could do it. Or if you did, you never let me know it, and you always paid the bill. Thank you.

To all the other sons and daughters out there, including my own, I hope you'll use this holiday to begin looking at life through a new lens. Instead of focusing on what could have been better, I hope you'll train your eyes to see how good it really was and continues to be.

Removing the black dot makes more room on the page for kindness.

Start Saying Yes to Kindness

I want to share a story with you, and then I want to share a story with you. The way they work together in one woman's life is breathtaking and contains a lesson for all of us.

Here's story No. 1, which is contained in this letter I got from a woman named Tammy Guffey.

"My husband and I got a call asking if we were renting our basement. Our plan was to eventually rent it out, but it needed a major gut job first.

The people inquiring were Rick and Mary. They had lost the contract on the house they were buying and needed a place to stay. They had already come up with dead ends through both their church and family.

My husband and I have been homeless before and know the feeling too well, so we told them they could have our bedroom and we would share our kids' room.

Rick and Mary insisted on staying in the one room of the torn up basement that was still intact. We quickly put a new vanity in the bathroom so they would have a sink, but we all shared the upstairs shower.

They moved in on a Saturday, the same day that we were leaving for a family vacation. These strangers watched our house, but I wasn't worried. I knew they would soon be our friends.

Rick and Mary only ended up staying about three weeks, but I was right, we became friends for life.

I was happy to help someone in a situation I had once been in myself, and I hope I never forget the lessons I learned during that time in my life or the importance of kindness."

At the bottom of Tammy's letter was a link to her website (yestokindness.com), which led me to her blog. That's when I found out that Tammy uses kindness for her battle with life like I used kindness during my battle with breast cancer.

Tammy suffers from bipolar depression and post-traumatic stress disorder. Here's story No. 2, which is how Tammy explains her disease.

"Have you ever wondered what could be so bad that someone could take their own life? I have struggled with suicidal thoughts since I was in junior high. Now 20 years later, in my 33rd year, the suicidal thoughts have built a super highway in my brain. Let me break that down for you.

When a person without a suicide super highway gets negative feedback, they brush it off, learn from it and move on. For me, I go right to 'I should kill myself.'

When a person without a suicide super highway gets in a fight with their family, they know it will pass, they learn from it and move on. For me, I go right to 'I should kill myself.'

When a person without a suicide super highway drops a glass and breaks it, they clean it up. For me, I go right to 'I should kill myself.'

It's not in a poor me, I need attention, nobody loves me kind of way.

It's real. It's scary. It's overwhelming.

On Aug. 11, Robin Williams will have been gone for two years. That same exact day one year earlier was the last time I attempted suicide. I feel like I need a sticker.

Everyday I battle this. Every moment I have to distract myself from this and I never know what will be the trigger. So when I call you to see if I can help you, I'm probably just needing a break from myself. It's not always about you, so please say yes."

Tammy has found that the best way to get out of her own mind and escape those dark thoughts is by being kind. She reaches out to others and offers her kindness as a means of survival.

Many of us say no to people who want to help us paint a room or weed a garden or taxi children simply because we think we're being a burden on them. Tammy gives us new insight into other reasons people offer their time. Perhaps we need to stop being so hesitant to say yes to kindness.

***Note: The National Suicide Prevention Lifeline is available 24 hours a day. Please call 1-800-273-8255 if you are having suicidal thoughts.

Where Does Kindness End?

I'm just the lady who writes about kindness. That's it. I'm not a social worker, educator or social activist. Yet, I'm often called to help in situations in which I feel totally helpless.

I was in school the other day when I spotted a kindergartner walking through the breakfast line. She saw me and her eyes lit up. After a big hug, she stepped back and solemnly said, "Miss Nicole, when I was waiting for the bus this morning, my mom pulled me back into the house and slapped my face a bunch of times." As I looked at her delicate skin, I thought I could see one side that was still looking red and raw.

My heart broke. I wanted to scoop her up and bring her home with me to live happily ever after. Instead, I directed this hurting child to her teacher who was better equipped to handle the situation.

As I saw the little girl walk away holding her teacher's hand, it was all I could do not to yell after her, "You are precious! You are valuable! Someone you love is very, very sick, but that doesn't mean there is anything wrong with you!"

I got a long white envelope in the mail the other day. On the front in bold black letters were the words "Mailed from a Correctional Facility." It's not the first time I've gotten a letter from prison. Usually it's from an inmate who wants to share a kindness story, but this time, it was from a woman who wanted help.

In a seven-page handwritten letter, she spelled out her story. She is awaiting trial for meth trafficking and a gun charge. While she admits to being a previous drug user, she says she is innocent of these particular crimes.

She went on to say that she had been working undercover on the Federal Task Force when she and her husband came across a 10-year-old child drugged up on heroin and nodding off in a car. She went on to give me specific locations and names of people involved in meth trafficking, child trafficking and a horrifying child brothel.

This is not in a seedy area of Los Angeles or a crime-filled neighborhood in New York. This woman says she saw these atrocities in western North Dakota. She wants me to help prove her innocence on these latest charges so she can continue fighting for the children who are being held captive.

Now, let's just take a break from the heaviness for a moment so I can speak to the part of your brain that is perhaps saying, "Yeah right. She's a con artist." Maybe you're even thinking of the little girl who said her momma slapped her and assuming kids exaggerate. I'm not judging. Those thoughts have floated across my mind, too.

But. There is always a but.

But what if they are telling the truth? What if a child is being abused and I gave her a hug and said, "Oh sweetie, go back to class. It'll be OK." Or what if there are children being sold for sex in rural North Dakota and I didn't say anything?

Am I exempt because I'm not qualified to deal with these issues? Where does kindness start and where does it get to stop?

I've been wrestling with these issues. Maybe you have, too.

Here's the best advice I can give myself: Not every commission is my mission.

I have to choose to fiercely love and protect and show kindness to those in my particular mission field. When a call comes from another field, I have to do my best to alert others who are working in that particular area.

In these cases, that includes teachers and police. I've passed along the letter from the prison to several people who probably won't be as shocked to receive it as I was. This is their mission field.

I haven't heard how the story ended and I probably never will.

I love kindness, and while I have ideas of how to use it in our lives, I'm certainly not the expert on the subject. I'd love to hear your thoughts on better ways to handle these sorts of situations so we can all learn from each other.

Please join me online with your comments at www.facebook.com/NicoleJPhillips.

Calming Anxiety with Kindness

We're coming upon a season of great celebration. My mailbox is full of pictures of fresh young faces excited to begin a new chapter of life. You can see by the twinkle in their eyes that they are looking forward to saying goodbye to cafeteria lunches and study halls.

Parents are frantically sweeping out garages and hunting down folding tables in preparation for the parties.

But that's not all. As soon as we get past graduation, we head straight into the peak wedding month. What did I say? A season of celebration!

I happen to love parties—when I get to be in control of them. I'm a bit of an introverted extrovert, which means I'm happy to be surrounded by people, but I don't want to just stand there talking. Or maybe that makes me an extroverted introvert. Either way, I want to be the person greeting guests or passing out punch or grilling burgers on the back porch. OK, not the grilling part. I hate to cook.

Anyway, it makes me very nervous and uncomfortable to walk into a social situation without a specific purpose. Perhaps you can relate. It doesn't have to be a graduation party or mammoth wedding. It can be a training seminar or a school concert or really anything that requires me to mingle before the main event.

As I love to remind my kids, whenever there's a problem, kindness is the solution. But how could kindness possibly be incorporated into this scenario? It's not like I'm going to bring party gifts to pass out to 100 of my closest strangers.

Several years ago, I stumbled upon some incredible advice while watching a teaching DVD called "Becoming More Than a Good Bible Study Girl" by Lysa TerKeurst.

I found one nugget of wisdom so true, so powerful and so kind that I've implemented it into every social situation since.

Here it goes. Maybe it'll work for you, too.

Let's say you walk into a party and start feeling overwhelmed because everyone is wearing a dress and you're wearing jeans. Or perhaps it looks like everyone is there with a date and you're single. Or maybe it seems as if everyone knows everyone and you know no one. That's when you begin the hunt.

Look for the person in the room who looks more uncomfortable than you. Often they will be in the corner and have a wide-eyed "deer in the headlights" sort of look about them. Walk up, smile and introduce yourself.

I find that I am immediately empowered by this small, subtle act of kindness.

All of a sudden, I have a job. I am "the kind one" who is there to help other people have a good time. I seem to instantly forget that 30 seconds ago I was feeling terrified, self-conscious and out of place.

I remember being at a church function for my kids a few summers ago. We had just moved into town the month before, so when I walked into the banquet hall, there were no familiar faces. Standing alone next to a table was a woman who was quite a bit older than me. It was very evident that she was not in her comfort zone.

While it initially appeared that we had nothing in common, I quickly found out she was the guardian of her grandchildren, and that our kids were in the same grade and would be attending the same school in the fall. I gained a new friend that day, simply by walking over and saying "hi," and we both had a better time than we thought we would.

Even if you're a person who relishes the social scene, I hope you'll give this kindness challenge a try. Whether you're a wallflower or the life of the party, it always feels good to help others.

Kindness Beats Bullying

I was sitting in my basement a few weeks ago with tears streaming down my face.

The room was dark except for the glow of the television. It was a Saturday night and I was four days out from my reconstructive surgery. Something was wrong. The pain was more intense than anything I had ever experienced in my life. No medication would touch it. I had no choice but to sit very still all night long and ring the bell at my side when I needed my husband to help me make the excruciating trip to the bathroom. I was waiting for Monday when the doctor would remove the plastic tube in my side that was sitting on a raw nerve.

Needing a distraction from late-night TV, I opened my computer to check emails. That's when I found a letter from a 14-year-old girl in South Florida named Juliette Valle. She had stumbled across my most recent kindness column.

"Dear Nicole, I recently saw your article about #kindawesome and what you did with the KIND bars. I want to do something similar. I am the current Miss Broward County's Outstanding Teen 2016. In June I will try for the Miss Florida Teen crown.

My platform is 'Kindness is Key' which stems from my personal experience with bullying.

It began on the first day of eighth grade when my friends since age 5 began to exclude me from everything, including editing me out of pictures of the first day of school and telling me there was no room at the lunch table. It grew to calling me on FaceTime to let me know there were parties I wasn't invited to. Going to school each day was hard.

By talking to a local specialist in teen bullying, I learned my authentic voice was one of kindness.

I am not the 'fight back' type and so I began to pursue being kind every day and helping defend others from the bullying I would witness, mainly with younger students.

It kept me so busy and made me so happy, that the year flew by.

While I cannot say I never noticed my own continual bullying by exclusion, I was able to make many other friends through my 'kindness experiment.'

The next year, I joined the high school Kindness Club. It was started a few years before by an older girl from my dance studio.

In this club we hold conferences to teach girls from area middle and high schools that kindness and inclusion trump bullying.

At our first conference, the team leaders asked the club members to stand up and share our own personal experiences with bullying.

When it was my turn, I described my eighth-grade year. Girls who went to grade school with me (but were not part of the bullies) were shocked. I could see they had no idea.

One of the most striking things about that night was when a girl a year older than me stood up to relate her story.

I had always admired her.

She was the eighth-grade valedictorian and was very popular.

She said one day I stopped her in high school to compliment her socks. Our socks are our only means of expression in my school, as we wear a specific uniform and shoes.

She said she cried when her mother picked her up because someone had noticed her and said a kind word.

I was stunned. I am still stunned as I write this, that a small compliment to this kind of superstar meant so much.

Because of that story, I'm now obsessed with being kind and complimenting people sincerely, whether it is their earrings, their performance in dance class or a perfectly done winged eye.

This month, I will return to my grade school to speak to the fourth-grade girls about kindness as an antidote to bullying. I feel like I have come full circle.

My mom says she will buy me some KIND bars to hand out. I plan on attaching handwritten notes with the Aesop quote 'No act of kindness, no matter how small, is ever wasted.' Just like you did."

Thank you for bravely sharing your story, Juliette. Your sweet email came in the midst of my own personal darkness, and like kindness always does, it took the attention off of my own pain and reminded me to look for the light.

Saying Goodbye to My Kindergartners

If I don't write this down, I know I'll forget it. I don't want to forget. I want to remember Tuesday for the rest of my life.

Tuesday was the day I went into my son's kindergarten class for the last time.

Ben's teacher has given me 30 minutes in the classroom each week for a mini-session I affectionately refer to as "KinderKindness." Thirty minutes in a classroom with kindergartners is an incredibly valuable amount of time—equivalent to buying a 30-second commercial during the Super Bowl for $5 million. (Seriously, that's what it costs. I just looked it up.)

These kids are busy learning big lessons like how to read, how to subtract, and how to stand in line without touching anyone else. Trust me, Mrs. H. uses every minute of the day to prepare them for first grade and for life. Thirty minutes a week for an entire year was a huge gift.

I rushed into the school on Tuesday, five minutes late. I hate to be late. Hate it. I had a good excuse, but it doesn't matter. Twenty-three kids and three adults were waiting on me, and I was letting them down. Not very kind.

I scurried through the hall, but when I got to the kindergarten area, the room was black. All the lights were out and it was totally silent. The kids were gone. They had left for recess or art or gym and I had missed them.

Mrs. H. stepped out of the darkness as I sputtered out an explanation. "I'm so sorry ..."

"No worries," she said. "They should be back in a few minutes. Come on in, I'll turn on the lights."

As I stepped into the classroom and the fluorescent bulbs snapped on, 23 of the sweetest smiling faces excitedly yelled, "Surprise!"

My first thought was, "Oh no! I just made 23 kids sit quietly in the dark for an extra five minutes." And then I thought, "Wow! They did it! They actually sat quietly enough in the dark to surprise me. I'm so proud of them!"

The quietness was long gone as the kids bubbled with enthusiasm to show me the card they had written for my last KinderKindness visit. Precious.

I re-read them the first book we'd ever read together, *Have You Filled A Bucket Today?* by Carol McCloud. Then we counted all the hearts they had collected and taped to the back wall: 301. Each heart represents an act of kindness the children either did or noticed.

One by one, the students came up and gave me a big hug or a high five for kindness (or both) and then got a treat bag filled with kindness coins and chocolate kisses. Some kids wanted to come back for one last extra hug. Again, precious.

That night, I asked Ben about his Glad, Sad and Act of Kindness for the day. He said his Glad was that I came into the school, and that he didn't have a Sad that day. "No tears?" I prompted. "Well," he said, "I almost had tears when I hugged you goodbye because it was your last Kindness day."

And then he remembered that he lives with me, so we weren't actually saying goodbye. I love kindergartners.

Kindness Ninja Promotes School Revolution

Brian Williams was supposed to be a high-powered, highly paid businessman. In college, he was ranked as the top business student in the country, as in the *entire* United States. Only, when he got out into the real world, he found he wasn't crazy about some of the shadier practices happening behind the scenes.

Now, just to be clear, I'm not talking about Brian Williams, the former "NBC Nightly News" anchor. I'm talking about Brian Williams, the Kindness Ninja.

Long before Brian dreamed of earning six figures, he dreamed of earning his black belt. Along with learning to flip, kick and chop, Brian learned that kindness is the ultimate form of self-defense.

Brian moved back to his hometown of Reno, Nev., in 2007 when his father was diagnosed with an autoimmune disease. Spending time with his family members, nine of whom are teachers, helped Brian re-evaluate his priorities and the impact he wanted to have on the world.

Brian took his expertise in marketing and began to plan. By October 2008, he was ready to unveil Think Kindness to a group of students at a school in Nevada. In that assembly, Brian issued a challenge: 5,000 acts of kindness in 15 days.

Today, he issues the same challenge all over the United States.

Using jokes and martial arts and competition with other schools, Brian creates a revolution of kindness that spans the whole community.

Once Brian is gone, the Kindness Crew, a group of students that is in on the ground floor, works to keep the momentum going.

Brian says the impact is both external and internal. "When you ask a child to recognize every time they hold a door open or pick up a pencil, they will instantly begin to notice all the people who do those things for them."

Because school hours are so limited with so much for kids to learn, the message fits the social and emotional learning standards (SEL), with a different kindness focus each day.

Students in the United States seem to be benefiting from Think Kindness (the schools report a 32 percent decrease in bully-related incidents), but young people on the other side of the globe are being affected as well.

That's because when Brian takes his program to middle and high schools, he makes it personal. He introduces the students to kids like Grace.

Grace lives in Kenya. She lost her mother and her father, and was sold into slavery by her grandmother at age 9. She's 22 now and is pursuing a social work degree with hopes of running an orphanage someday. Grace was allowed to begin her education only because she was given a pair of shoes. No shoes, no school. No school, no education. No education, well, I think you can imagine how that would have played out.

Thanks to the wonder of the Internet, students in the U.S. can communicate on their own with Grace and other kids in her community. They become friends on Facebook, and all of a sudden the world becomes a whole lot smaller.

Brian says he is always touched by the tears he sees running down the faces of American teenagers, even the boys, when they learn about what their peers in Africa are facing.

That's when he issues the challenge: Find them shoes. Lots and lots of shoes.

The first time, he challenged three schools to work together to collect 5,000 pairs of gently used shoes. They ended up with 8,000. To date, 200,000 pairs of shoes have been collected. Brian has been to Africa with students and teachers nine times to deliver shoes and carry out global acts of kindness. Grace has gotten to visit the U.S. to meet some of her online friends face-to-face.

Based on how far Think Kindness has come since 2008, I'd say Brian is putting his marketing background to good use. I'm certain he would have eventually found a more suitable fit had he decided to stay in the business world, but as a parent and lover of kindness, I'm sure glad he didn't.

Learn more about Brian's mission at ThinkKindness.org.

A Vision of Kindness

Imagine waking up Monday morning, ready for the work commute, but instead of sliding into your car, you slid into a pair of sneakers? You would walk out your front door and be greeted by everyone else in the neighborhood because no one was driving. You were all walking the five to 10 miles to work.

Can you imagine the conversations that would happen during those commutes? Can you imagine the joys and the sufferings that would be shared? Or the ideas that would blossom?

It sounds like a far-fetched scenario, but it's pretty realistic for a man in Washington named Dylan Raines. He is an Earth Pilgrim. He walks everywhere he goes. The other day he walked to the Seattle Space Needle.

It was a 16-mile trek to raise money for water wells in South Sudan, but when he got to the Space Needle, it was blurry. Most things in Dylan's life are blurry. He's nearly blind.

Dylan's corneas are misshapen. Ironically he didn't find out until he was 16 and went in to apply for a driver's license. Once he reached his early 20s, he knew his driving days were over, so he began relying on his feet.

Today, Dylan says the vision in his right eye is nearly gone, but he can see large objects, like cars, with his left eye. He can't see road signs until he's close to them, but he does have glasses that help him use his computer so he can continue his work as a freelance Web designer.

While Dylan's physical vision is impaired, his spiritual vision is crystal clear.

"I've never seen my vision as a disability because it has shown me the beauty of walking. My other senses are heightened. It's hard for me to judge someone on how they look, so I see things differently. I enjoy that, so I don't see this as a disability or as something that has hampered me in life."

Dylan now walks to raise awareness for causes to help transform the lives of people he believes are in the greatest need. Several times a week he walks 15 to 20 miles for causes related to food, water, shelter and adoption.

In March of 2016, he walked 100 miles, from Seattle to Canada, to raise awareness and funds to restore water wells in South Sudan. In May, he walked another 100 miles to raise money to help people pay for adoptions through Liberty Adoption Advocates (libertyscall.org).

Dylan's first major walk was in April 2015 when he walked 1,000 miles along parts of the California coast and the entire Oregon coast.

It was a big unplanned adventure at the time, but the idea of changing the world was birthed step by step through that journey.

Dylan carries a backpack, tent and sleeping bag everywhere he goes and usually stays at state parks or churches, speaking along the way, both to groups of people and to individuals, like the desperate and downtrodden man he met one night at a campground.

The man's wife and son had both died, and the man felt hopeless. In a great act of kindness, Dylan spoke life into that man's soul.

The next morning, they went for coffee and found the man a place to live.

Dylan says, "It's not about what I can do, but what we can do together. Walking is the first big step toward building community. As we strengthen communities we become aware of how we can help others who are suffering."

Dylan has set up an organization called Earth Pilgrim (earthpilgrim.net). It is a global NGO (nongovernmental organization) with a mission to inspire people to walk wherever they live for the causes and projects they believe are working to make a better world for us all.

"I'm a traveler and I'd love to connect with people and help them unearth their passion and the impact they want to have in the world."

Dylan walks in rain, sleet and snow, but he's not a huge fan of scorching summer days. He's got a long list of places he hopes to explore on foot. Maybe you'd like to join him.

"It's so easy to make someone just a little happier and it sure makes me happier."

We Are All Human

I ordered chicken tenders at the pool last summer for my kids. We are clearly not foodies (or we wouldn't have ordered chicken tenders in the first place), but this meal was inedible. The poor little freezer-burned then overcooked nuggets barely resembled food.

My kids were disappointed, but happy to eat french fries for lunch, so I let it go. I did not complain. I did not send them back. I didn't even tell the college girl at the concession stand that there was a problem.

My girlfriend sitting next to me was stunned. "Why don't you send them back?" she asked. I took a moment to look around at all of the children happily flitting back and forth between eating and swimming. We had ordered chicken tenders 20 other times at that same pool and never had a problem, but today was different. The pool was full of kids, and the one worker at the concession stand was overwhelmed. She didn't need me to remind her that this was not her best day.

I turned back to my friend and said, "She's here, working, and I'm sitting in the sun, relaxing. Life is good for me. I don't know what it's like for her right now."

There are times when I feel compelled to get my money's worth, but there are also times when I don't.

Each situation is different, and this time, I just wanted to let it go and enjoy the day.

Besides, when my kids eat too many chicken tenders, they don't have room for ice cream, and it was definitely an ice cream kind of day.

A North Dakota woman who wished to remain anonymous shared a story with me that reminded me of that day at the pool.

"Quite a few years ago at noon in Valley City, North Dakota I ordered a hamburger with pickles, no ketchup or mustard, exactly the way I always order it. The waitress brought it with everything on it. I pointed out the error and when she brought out the new burger topped correctly I tried to give the wrong one back. She said, 'Just keep it,' quite curtly, and stalked off.

"I enjoyed my new burger, sort of, then noticed her angrily wiping tables and thought to myself, 'It's ridiculous that I should have upset her so over a darn hamburger,' so I went over and apologized for my miscommunication. She smiled wanly and said, 'I'm getting married at 4 at the courthouse.'

"Imagine that poor girl getting off work and heading downtown to get married! I guess she was a little distracted! I gave her a hug and wished her well and we both felt lighter-hearted.

"It's so easy to make someone just a little happier and it sure makes me happier."

There are certainly times when we need to speak up for our preferences. But sometimes, instead of focusing on how we've been slighted, it helps to focus on the other person and perhaps remind ourselves that we are all human.

Only Kindness Matters

I have a picture on my office wall that says, "Kindness Matters." The coffee cup on my desk reminds me to "Be Kind."

I'm naturally drawn to things that revolve around kindness, whether it's artwork or the latest academic research.

When a radio announcer mentions kindness, my ears perk up. But it hasn't always been this way.

My husband heard a song on the radio the other day and picked up the phone. "Hey, I found your true soulmate. It's Jewel."

Hmmm. I hadn't ever thought of Jewel as my soulmate. I kind of thought my husband was my one true partner. "OK, I'm listening," I hesitantly replied.

"She has this song, and it says, 'In the end, only kindness matters' and then there's this line that says, 'I will get down on my knees, and I will pray.' It's like you wrote the song, Nic! It's totally your anthem."

I assured my husband that I am not a ghostwriter for Jewel, then I went home and Googled the song.

It's called *Hands*, and it was released in 1998.

If I had written that song based on my beliefs in the late '90s, I'm sad to say, it would have included the line, "In the end, only Nicole matters."

I was Miss Wisconsin that year, and after competing in the Miss America pageant, I spent the year touring the state talking to kids about how to deal with crisis, primarily divorce.

My big line was, "No matter where you come from, no matter what's happened to you in the past, from here on out, you get to make the decisions that determine your future."

Not bad advice, because it's true that we can't spend our lives dwelling on the past or on other people's mistakes, but looking back, I see it also wasn't necessarily good advice.

I left out one major aspect. Kindness. What is the point of succeeding in this life if you step on everyone else's head when you climb up the ladder? You'll get to the top, still feeling empty, and realize you're no better than the people who hurt you.

I wish I wouldn't have ended there when I talked to those students. I wish I would have continued on and reminded them that the only way to truly create joy in your life is by creating joy in the lives of others.

I probably would have had to convince them that it's not hard and it's not scary (although sometimes it is). I would have assured them, as I assure you now, that kindness will not cause bankruptcy financially, emotionally or physically.

It's just a matter of teaching yourself to think, "What can I do to brighten the day of the person standing in front of me?"

You don't even have to go out looking for people to help.

You may be in line at the gas station and notice the clerk has a warm, beautiful smile. Instead of just thinking it, say it!

You don't know what kind of path that person is walking, but if it's anything like the rest of ours, it's occasionally bumpy.

If you are the one who can smooth it out, even for a moment, it will be worth it for both of you.

I'm touched that my husband would hear a song about kindness and think of me. A lot has changed since 1998. Thank God.

Signs of Kindness From Above

My friend, Ann, finds pennies in the strangest places. She even found one in the tiny skull skeleton of a squirrel in her yard. Skull skeleton of a squirrel—try saying that 10 times fast.

I'm sure I wrinkled my nose and shrieked, "Gross!" when she told me, but to Ann, it wasn't gross at all. It was beautiful.

Everything about finding that penny that day in that particular way reminded her of her son, Matt, who died when he was 23 years old. She felt like he was saying, "Mom, it's OK."

I can understand the beauty in that. Every time I find a penny hiding somewhere unexpected, I think of God. Pennies from heaven. They remind me that God sees me and loves me and is way bigger than any problem I'm facing.

Sunday is Easter. It's a time to rejoice, knowing that Jesus not only paid for our sins, but he also overcame hell for each of us who turns to him. Heaven awaits, but that doesn't always make life easier in the here and now when we are missing someone we love.

Barbara Trieglaff lost her 48-year-old daughter, Lisa Jahnke, almost two years ago. She says there were so few resources for kids on coping after a loss that her other daughter, Kara Scheer, felt compelled to write a children's book.

The Whisper of a Firefly encourages families to find comfort in the signs they may see after losing a loved one.

Stephanie Astrup of Fargo, North Dakota provided the delightful, whimsical illustrations, and there are several pages in the book where children can add their own artwork.

Barbara says looking for signs is a powerful tool for helping people survive after a loss.

"Our daughter, Lisa, was a teacher in the gifted program at Fargo Public Schools until cancer took her in June 2014.

While there was an outpouring of love at the time of the illness and again during the funeral, there is nothing that can prepare you for the days afterward when you realize that she's really gone and we have to find a way to cope without her.

In the days and weeks following Lisa's death, we had family get-togethers that always led to memories of Lisa.

Soon we realized we weren't just sharing memories, but more than that. We were experiencing signs."

Many of those signs are included in the book, including one especially meaningful to Barbara.

"We built a house, planted trees and waited several years for the beautiful eastern bluebirds to make a home in our yard, but they just wouldn't come.

The night before she died, I whispered to Lisa, 'See what you can do about the bluebirds.' She whispered back that she would try.

The next morning, Lisa was gone, but in the apple tree were two bluebirds."

My heart is hurting for Barb, Kara, my friend Ann and all of you who have lost someone too soon.

I want you to know, I am praying for you, that this Easter brings you a peace and joy that is beyond understanding, and that God fills your day with signs of how much you are loved.

The Whisper of a Firefly can be purchased online on Amazon.

Kindness and Cellphones to the Rescue

I'm about to share one of my not-so-great parenting moments. I'm pretty sure I'm at fault, but I refuse to ask the experts because I'm afraid of the verbal lashing I'll get.

Luckily, the kindness and common sense of a stranger kept my kids from any real danger.

Last January, I decided to be a brave mom and I took my three kids to Walt Disney World in Florida. By myself. Now, honestly, my kids are 12, 10 and 5, so I figured as long as I kept an eye on the littlest one, we'd all be OK.

That was my mindset as the big kids were begging to go on big kid rides while the little one was refusing to do anything more adventurous than ride the boat around "It's a Small World."

I told the two older kids to hit one quick ride and then meet me in *this exact spot*. Ben and I would stand there and wait for them.

And wait we did.

What was taking them so long?

About 45 minutes later, my cellphone rang. I fumbled for it, but it ended up going to voicemail. No worries, it was a number I didn't recognize anyway.

Five minutes later, my phone rang again.

This time, I said "Hello" and heard the familiar, but frightened voice of my daughter, Jordan.

"Mom? Charlie and I couldn't find you at the meeting spot so we went into a store and the lady working here let me use her cellphone, and then she said we should stay in the store until you could come get us. So, we're at the Trading Post. Are you mad?"

I hung up, grabbed Ben and ran.

They were safe at that point, so I don't know what the hurry was, but I suddenly had an overwhelming need to wrap my arms around my babies and assure them I hadn't abandoned them.

Thank goodness for a fast-thinking Disney employee and a daughter who knew where to go to ask for help.

North Dakota resident Judy Legge has also experienced a worker coming to the rescue with a cellphone. Although she didn't lose her children, she was certainly feeling the pinch of panic.

"On my way to a meeting, I stopped at Sam's Club in Fargo. In a hurry, I accidentally locked my keys in my vehicle.

'No problem,' I thought, 'I'll just call AAA.'

Well, there was a problem. I'd locked my phone in my vehicle, too.

Not knowing what to do next, I ran inside and asked the greeter if there was a phone somewhere. She offered me her personal cellphone so I could call right there at the door. The AAA guy said he'd be there in about 30 minutes. He said he'd call when he got close.

I hung up and realized I hadn't called from my phone—mine was still in the car!

The Sam's Club greeter told me to shop for the items I needed while she waited for the call.

I still think of that kind woman, who refused to take any payment for her good deed. Thanks to her, I ended up making it to my meeting on time. In her honor, I try to 'pass it on' whenever I can."

Boy, do I understand that feeling of gratitude and "passing it on" in response to someone's kindness.

When I got to the Trading Post at Disney, it was all I could do not to hug the woman who had helped my children.

She kindly kept an eye on my kids and perhaps with even more kindness, bit her tongue instead of reminding me not to let my offspring run around Disney World alone.

After-School Program Teaches Kids About Kindness

In a little town that doesn't get much press is a woman who quietly goes about the task of teaching kids.

Pamela Wiese is a truancy officer and paraprofessional at a school in Henning, Minnesota, a town of about 800 people.

I have no doubt she shows great compassion and empathy in the hours that fill most of her days. But I get the feeling her legacy will be left through an after-school program she leads every Tuesday and Thursday where she teaches kids about kindness.

"Where does kindness begin? With the youngest of us.

Last year, the theme in my room was about learning kindness and manners.

We have done many acts of kindness since that first day, including leaving sticky notes on all of the students' lockers, delivering conversation hearts on Valentine's Day, writing thank-you notes to our custodial and nutritional staffs, and even writing and performing our own play about why it is important to be kind and have manners.

We are continuing the theme again this year by stepping up to daily challenges.

I ask the students to perform an act of kindness and then journal about their experience. It really gets them thinking about what they can do without expecting anything in return.

The youngest students are in kindergarten, and the oldest are in eighth grade.

I have nearly 60 kids going through the classroom, so they are bound to touch a lot of people's lives in our little town."

This year, the kindness in Mrs. Wiese's classroom also includes a twist.

"We realized, until we are kind to ourselves, we can't show it to others. So, how are we kind to ourselves? By figuring out what we like and how we see ourselves.

We gave each student a silhouette shape of a boy or girl. Then we gave the children endless supplies of magazines and had them cut out pictures of things they thought described themselves.

We also drew out their names in bubble letters. They again had to skim the magazines and find adjectives that describe themselves. This was harder, but a lot more interesting. I have these hanging in the hallway, and they are so wonderful.

We have also been playing games that concentrate on speaking nicely.

First, everyone lines up and you have to say something nice about the person next to you before you pass the ball.

Then we time it.

Then we can't say anything that someone else has already said. It just keeps getting a little tougher and requiring a little more effort.

Then comes the big one: you can't pass the ball until you say something nice about yourself!

After that, we time it, and they can't say anything that someone else has already said. This has been challenging, but very rewarding. We play it often.

Later this month, the kids will put that self-esteem to good use as they take the stage for a talent show. Finding each of their hidden talents involved some soul searching, but the end result is going to be amazing.

The audience will see artists, hula-hoopers, jump-ropers, comedians, mathematicians, musicians, hair-braiders, dancers and taekwondo experts.

These kids need to feel kindness, not just know what the word means. We all have it in us, we just have to figure out how to get it out and share it. To have them understand the feeling they get from giving is so amazing."

Mrs. Wiese and her students are often given credit for acts of kindness in their community that they didn't actually do, which means the kindness is spreading. Or as I like to say, it's contagious.

Creating Kinder Thinking

I've been thinking a lot lately about what I've been thinking about. I don't know if this is the case for you, but my mind can follow a squirrel or bright shiny object into the next dimension in no time flat.

A friend recently told me she struggles with cooking because of attention deficit disorder. As soon as she steps away from the recipe to crack an egg or measure out a teaspoon of vanilla, she forgets what she was in the process of making. I feel her pain. And so does my family. Just ask them about the two times I've made lasagna and forgot to add the lasagna noodles.

The other night I made taco soup in the Crock-Pot. Beef, beans, corn, tomatoes ... Saul took one sniff and said, "Chili!" to which I quickly corrected him, "It's taco soup. I hate chili." Then my in-laws walked in, peeked in the Crock-Pot and proclaimed, "Chili!" It's taco soup, people ...

I digress. What was I talking about? Oh yeah. Thoughts.

When it's just a matter of getting confused in the kitchen, it's sort of funny, but sometimes I allow my brain to wallow in matters that are (at best) unproductive and (at worst) harmful to my mental health.

Do you ever find yourself role-playing an angry hypothetical argument about a situation that will probably never present itself in real life?

I stand in the shower and think, "If I get another telemarketing call, I am totally going to let them have it!"

Then I play out the whole conversation in my mind where I am smart and cutting and ... well, mean.

I have just chewed someone up in my thoughts and instead of emerging victorious, I end up feeling badly for something that never even happened.

I don't want to be someone who gets caught up in bitterness and resentment and ego. I want to be kind.

Maybe it's worry that overtakes your mind. That's a tough one, because there are so many options. You can worry about your health or your children or your neighbor or your finances or your neighbor's finances. I can spend hours mulling over what I would do if I found out I had cancer in the other breast. Yes, I come up with a whole game plan, but I've also just worked myself into such a state that I don't have the energy to do anything productive. I need a nap.

I've been studying a lot about thoughts lately. Joyce Meyer is one of the best authors I've come across when it comes to thinking.

Her book, *Battlefield of the Mind*, is one of my longtime favorites. Also on my bookshelf is *The Mind Connection: How the Thoughts You Choose Affect Your Mood, Behavior, and Decisions*, and two more books called *Power Thoughts* and *Change Your Words, Change Your Life: Understanding the Power of Every Word You Speak*.

Basically, it boils down to this: Realize you have the power to control your thoughts. I didn't believe it until I tried it, but boy, my world totally opened up several years ago when I first gave it a try.

For me, I simply started by thinking about my thoughts. When a thought entered my brain, I would either accept it or reject it.

I would literally say, "I reject that thought" when it was a worrying or wandering thought. If it didn't hold a specific purpose for positivity, I threw it out.

But here's the big thing — you have to decide ahead of time what you're going to use to replace your negative thoughts. You can't just tell them to go away without giving your mind a new, positive focus.

You may have to find your own replacement thought, but here was mine: "Love, joy, peace, patience, kindness, goodness, faithfulness, gentleness, self-control."

I memorized the fruits of the Spirit from the Bible (Galatians 5:22-23) and counted out all nine of them every time my brain wanted to worry.

It immediately calmed and preoccupied me until whatever negativity I was producing in my mind passed.

Here it is again: 1) Say, "I reject that thought." 2) Start thinking your predetermined replacement thought.

I'm forcing myself to follow these steps again, too. My world is filled with so much joy and peace that I often get complacent, so when a little bump in the road comes along, I allow my brain to stretch it way out of proportion or start running after some fictional scenario.

I need a tuneup, and since I was thinking of giving myself a talking-to, I thought I'd see if you needed one, too.

Kindness in a Kidney Donation

What's the furthest you would go for kindness? Do you even know? Maybe you'll give your time, but not your money. Maybe you'll give your money, but not your time. Maybe you'll give your time and money as long as you don't have to sacrifice your personal comfort.

It's humbling to realize our limitations, both the tangible ones and the ones we create in our minds.

Jeff Ficek has been dealing with a very real impediment. When he was 18, he was diagnosed with a type of arthritis that affects the lower back and hips. The medication that for years allowed him to live with a high quality of life came at a high price. It killed his kidneys. This past fall, Jeff's kidney function was down to 10-12 percent. He was tiring quickly, retaining water and in desperate need of a transplant.

Jeff's siblings, family members and some close friends were tested, but none of them came up as a match.

Then one day Jeff was out golfing. They say a lot gets done on the golf course, and this particular day was proof. That was the day Jeremy Gregoire, a fellow golfer, found out Jeff needed a kidney.

"We were out golfing, Jeff, myself and two others. As we were walking down the fairway, I casually asked Jeff how his health was going. He said nothing had really changed, but didn't make a big deal of it. Then a couple holes later, a friend said Jeff's not doing as well as he's letting on. That friend tried to donate a kidney, but wasn't a match, so I thought I'd call and see if I could get tested."

Jeremy ended up going to nearly a dozen appointments to determine if he was physically, emotionally and financially healthy enough to go through with the surgery.

"I didn't know it would be so complicated, but I went in thinking, 'If Jeff needs a kidney and I have one, why not?' "

Even as a person who loves kindness, I could think of a lot of reasons why I wouldn't want my husband to donate a kidney, but Jeremy's wife supported his decision.

She was right next to him on Dec. 21 when they told Jeff the good news: Jeremy was a match.

Jeff says it's a day he'll never forget.

"I was home sick that day. Jeremy said his wife was baking Christmas cookies and asked if they could stop by. Heidi and Jeremy came over at about 8 p.m.

We talked a bit, and then he handed me a gift bag with a can of kidney beans inside.

I was a little slow on the joke until Jeremy said, 'You and I are a match and we're doing the surgery on January 26th.'

It was a day that changed my life.

It was an incredible moment I will never forget. I'm so excited about the additional bond that we now have.

His gift of life is changing my life. There was a lot of uncertainty in my life and it's something I'll forever be grateful for. It's just so awesome.

My outlook on life is usually as a realist, but when you get a gift like that, you can't help but be excited about the future."

Both men are recovering well from the surgery and are back at work. While Jeff and Jeremy's lives have certainly been changed by this act of selflessness, I'm certain the friends and family who got to watch from the sidelines are also reconsidering their boundaries when it comes to kindness. In fact, Jeremy told me several of his friends have already offered to give up their kidneys in the future if he ever finds himself one short.

Broken Back Leads to Many Acts of Kindness

I love the way people look at me when I mention all the blessings that we experienced during my bout with breast cancer this past summer.

The love I felt from friends, strangers and even my own family far surpassed any act of kindness I had ever previously experienced.

I know this is a bold statement — and my husband may disagree — but I'm going to say it anyway: Going through cancer was worth it when I look at all of the kindness it brought into our lives.

I'm not sure if Hugh Culbertson is ready to say the same thing about his wife's back injury.

They are still in the process of healing, but I can tell by the letter he sent me that Hugh and his wife are definitely aware of and grateful for all the kindness surrounding them.

Here's what he had to say:

"On June 17, 2015, my wife, Charlene, and I were camping in Michigan's Upper Peninsula. In the late evening, Charlene went to our camper to get something.

She slipped on the first or second step and fell, breaking the second vertebra in her neck region. A piece of bone put pressure on her spinal cord, leaving her unconscious and without breath for several seconds.

Thanks to a fine emergency medical team, she was revived.

She underwent serious neck surgery two days later. This was followed by six weeks of intensive therapy at a world-class rehabilitation hospital, nine weeks at a skilled nursing facility in our hometown and about three months of home care. The latter process continues.

During the past eight months or so, we have received many acts of kindness, confirming the idea expressed by some scholars that disaster can bring out the best in people (as well as, sometimes, the worst).

When he saw her turning blue, our son-in-law, Brad, who was camping with us, applied cardiopulmonary resuscitation techniques that he had learned as a volunteer fireman.

With coaching by phone from paramedics who were on the way, he brought her back to consciousness and probably saved her life.

Also, rangers at the state park where we were staying kept our camper in their yard for several days as Charlene underwent surgery and other treatment some 85 miles away in Marquette, Michigan.

Our granddaughter and her husband then helped our daughter and son-in law drive our camper, pulled by a Suburban, the 800 miles or so to our home in Athens, Ohio.

When we arrived at the hospital, arrangements were made for me to stay with Charlene 24/7, sleeping on a cot in her room.

During that time, our son and daughter visited regularly.

My daughter often took me out to eat to give me a break from the hospital routine, and our son drove me the 70 miles from Athens to Columbus several times so I could make arrangements back home.

Our pastor visited many times, as did several friends from my workplace in the Ohio University School of Journalism and from our church. They brought gifts. They contributed food regularly to our home for several weeks after we left the hospital. They also offered to help in many other ways, including adorning Charlene's room with flowers while she was in the hospital and at the nursing home.

Perhaps most amazingly, our granddaughter signed on to help look after her 'granny' at home. Annie is a nursing student, so she was able to get a job with a home-care agency and look after her for five-six hours each weekday. Other home-care aides also come on occasion and show great sensitivity as they realize Charlene loves to chat.

Certainly the saying 'There is a silver lining in every cloud' surely holds true for us."

Thanks for sharing your story, Hugh. It is so difficult sometimes to see the silver lining in the midst of a storm, but looking for the kindness in a situation can help us bring it into view.

Miles and Miles of Kindness

There are certain things that will never be on my bucket list.

Skydiving. Every person I've ever known who has done it loves it. I'm not buying it.

Alligator wrestling. I've never met anyone who has done this, and there is probably a reason.

Finishing (or starting) an Ironman race. That's where you swim a lot, bike a lot and then run a full marathon. No thank you.

I'm certainly not done exploring and jumping into new adventures, but those three things are off the list. They require a certain physical and mental toughness that I don't possess and I'm not interested in pursuing.

That said, I have a lot of respect for people who do really hard things.

My friend Jessica has never jumped out of an airplane or gone one-on-one with an alligator, but she has started (and finished) an Ironman. She's also done 12 marathons, but who's counting?

Oh, have I mentioned she has five kids?

Jessica loves to challenge her body and she loves kindness, so for her 40th birthday last week, she ran 40 miles. In one day. She started at 4:32 a.m. and ran on and off until 3:45 p.m. She had to take a break from 7 to 10 a.m. so she could get her kids ready for school and wait for the baby sitter to show up.

At one point in the day, when she had to stop for water, she ran into a college student who didn't hide the fact that he thought she might be missing a few marbles. "What are you doing this for?" he asked, and then immediately followed it up with, "Lady, that is so crazy!"

But Jessica is not crazy. She's kind. Very, very kind.

Jessica wanted to celebrate her 40th birthday by doing two things she loves: running and showering people with kindness.

For months before the big day, Jessica had been stockpiling gift cards and jewelry and mittens and lots of other odds and ends, all with the idea of collecting 40 things that she could drop off in mailboxes along the route of her run.

She didn't take any credit for the generosity, she just delivered each gift with a note that said, "No act of kindness (no matter how small) is ever wasted." — Aesop

When my neighbor tried to thank me for anonymously giving her a $50 Amazon gift card, I had to giggle. "I didn't give it to you, but I think I know who did," I replied.

All day long people were treated to kindness: coffee for the teachers (that one she had delivered since she couldn't run with an urn on her back), blueberry bars for a class of triathletes, pizza gift cards for the bike shop staff and even a few things for her own family.

Many of the gifts she left in mailboxes, but some she gave away face-to-face. One interaction in particular really touched Jessica's heart.

There was a young couple, who looked like they were just out of high school, standing outside their trailer home working on a motorcycle. Jessica was in a pinch and needed to change clothes, so she paused her run to ask if they would let her use their bathroom. The young woman walked her into the house. On the way out, Jessica handed her a sizable gift card and thanked her for her kindness. Then she took off again on her run.

Jessica could tell that the gift was needed and would be greatly appreciated. Thinking about that moment fueled the rest of the run.

My friend only has one regret from the day. She says she wished she would have stayed to see that woman and a few others open their gifts. Not to get thanks or praise, but to experience the excitement that comes from watching a face light up and knowing you made it happen.

Jessica has put on miles and miles of kindness. It started long before her run began, and it will continue long after she's done running for good. She's just that kind of person; a person who sees possibility and turns it into reality, for herself and for others.

Now that her 40th is out of the way, Jessica says she's looking to the future. She's thinking of biking 41 miles for her 41st birthday next year, with many stops along the way for kindness, of course.

Let Down Your Guard for Kindness

A man knocked on my door during the last snowstorm. It was 8 o'clock at night and I was home alone with the kids. We were all snuggled on the couch in our jammies waiting for bedtime when I heard the dog begin to bark ferociously, followed by the sound of knocking.

I looked at the kids to see if they were expecting an evening guest and forgot to inform me, but they looked back with big, startled eyes. No one ever knocks on our door after dark. Ever.

As I looked out the front-door window, I spied a big man who was definitely a stranger. Instead of opening the door, I yelled, "Can I help you?" He yelled back from the front step, "Need your driveway plowed?"

I gave him a resolute, "No" and he disappeared back into his truck.

He may have just been a guy out looking to make an extra buck off the storm, but I don't know that. All I know is that for the rest of the night, my momma-bear instincts were on high alert and I slept with one eye open.

Sometimes it works that way in the daylight, too, with kindness. My efforts to make someone's day are met with suspicion, or I shut a well-meaning outsider down before they have a chance to help me because I'm afraid of getting hurt.

In the case of the nighttime snowstorm, I know I did the right thing by refusing to open the door to a stranger. But what about in safer, more public situations?

I've been exchanging emails with an amazing artist/musician whose latest music video, "Man on Wire," demonstrates how afraid we are sometimes to interact with others. His name is Doug Andrews and here's what he had to say about the day he shot the video:

"For the video, I dressed up as a street performer and initially intended on wandering the streets of Hamburg, Germany, playing for anyone who would listen. I had no idea where it would lead.

Most people ended up ignoring me and kept their distance, unable to see past my appearance. I felt invisible, like a ghost.

Spontaneously, I bought some flowers and passed them out to strangers. I could see the wheels turning in each person's mind as they tried to figure out if I expected something from them in return.

The moment they realized that I was simply giving them something without any expectation of getting something in return, they transformed and I could just feel their appreciation.

This simple act of kindness gave me great insight into everyday life.

We all want to be appreciated and noticed. It's so easy to reach out and connect with one another, but we rarely do it.

It took dressing up in a clown costume to realize that we are all wearing costumes every day, longing for someone to see through them and connect with the people we truly are.

There was a particular moment that day that stood out for me. You can see it in the video with the last flower I handed to a homeless man.

The moment I handed him the flower and we made eye contact, I saw a light in his eyes shining brightly.

I thought, 'Even if nothing else happens with this video, that one moment was worth everything.' Just a moment to brighten this man's day which he probably doesn't experience often.

It's actually very easy to do good in the world. You don't have to start an orphanage or dedicate your life and career to some enormous worthy cause (although that is also great!).

A smile, opening a door, or anonymously paying for someone's cup of coffee can make an enormous difference in someone's day and start a chain reaction.

One simple act of random kindness can change a life and, in effect, change the world."

Thanks for sharing your behind-the-scenes thoughts with us, Doug, and encouraging us to let down our guards enough to let in some kindness.

"More kindness,
more smiles."

Mother's Kindness Ripples Far

There is a woman in my town who does a lot of good. I mean A LOT. She and her husband have been blessed with a successful local business, and they are constantly pouring into the community. The thing is, they do it so quietly, unless you're really paying attention and perhaps digging a little, you'd never know the identities of the "anonymous" donors.

I happen to take a special interest in kindness and those who are radically loving others, both openly and incognito. I remember the kind things I hear people doing because I want to try out their ideas. Their kindness is contagious.

Many months ago, I got a card from this wonderfully giving woman. On the front was the Wonder Woman logo and inside was a pack of Wonder Woman postage stamps and a beautiful note.

The first part of the note said this:

"In honor of my mom, my personal Wonder Woman, on Mother's Day 2017, I've decided to acknowledge one woman a week for a year. My mom has always been one to build you up, yet keep you humble. She can do it all, yet never seems inconvenienced. She thinks of others first … always! She treats all people the same. She recognizes and celebrates the goodness in everyone.

Every time you use one of these stamps, I hope you remember that you are admired for your wonderful traits!"

I was wowed by the way this woman was honoring the kindness of her mom by showing kindness to others.

That would have been enough, but below that typed explanation was a handwritten greeting that said this:

"Dear Nicole,

I'm pretty sure you have super powers! I am constantly amazed at the goodness in your heart that you share with everyone!

You are in a position and have life experiences that make a lot of women aloof or unavailable to some women, yet you remain as humble as anyone I know.

I believe that comes from your faith and the belief that God's teaching that all of our life experiences, good and bad, are opportunities to grow and spread God's love.

Thanks for being an example to us all."

You guys. Those words. Wow. Who gets to hear such messages of affirmation from someone who is nearly a total stranger? I felt beyond blessed and was more adamant than ever that I wanted to pass along this type of encouragement to another.

Then I started thinking maybe other people would want to put this sort of kindness into action too.

I reached out to the woman who sent me the card and asked for permission to share it.

She responded by saying, "It's funny that your message comes when it does because I have been gathering up the texts, emails and thank you cards that I received from this project.

I have printed them out and am putting them in a pretty box to give to Mom for Mother's Day.

My hope is that she can see the impact she has made on others with her kindness, as this is where this whole project originated."

This may have begun with a project to honor a special mom, but I'm certain the ripples will continue to spread far beyond one family.

Just Love Them. And Pray.

I used to pray, "Please God, make me into the mom these kids deserve." I had three young, healthy, exuberant kids. They were thriving despite the fact that their mom was floundering.

That was seven years ago.

Today, those kids are 8, 12 and 14.

God's done a work in me that only God could do. If I ever doubted His existence, which I did, I doubt it no longer. Only God could transform my entire life — my mind, my marriage, my morals — the way they've been transformed.

But lately, instead of praying, "make me into the mom these kids deserve," I've found myself praying, "HELP!"

I'm scared. The stakes are high. I remember my attitude as a pre-teen and young adult. I was invincible. Rules were meant to curb my enthusiasm. And everyone who wasn't for me was against me.

So now, I look at my kids and realize that even if they don't have the gigantic chip on their shoulders that I did, some of their classmates do. And those peers are the people they are hanging out with 8 hours a day, trying to emulate, looking for approval from. These kids are good, sweet kids, but some of them are hurting and some of them are just stuck in the mindset that I was at that age.

My husband and I spent the weekend having long conversations about cellphones and social media. First we talked with each other, then we talked with our kids. They are by no means out of control, but some tweaking is sometimes necessary. (Not to be confused with twerking, which is never necessary.)

Anyway, I say that to say this. I'm wondering if you've ever had a near panic attack wondering if your kids are going to make it through. Whether they are little kids, medium kids or big kids, I think our parenting hearts never fully release. If that's you, maybe this prayer I keep recycling will help you the way it helps me when I mistakenly believe I'm in control.

Here it is:

"God, you created them. You are their original parent. As much as I love them, I know that you love them more than I ever could. So I thank you that I can trust you to take care of them in ways that I cannot."

As desperately as my control-freak instincts want to wrap them up in foam blocks and follow them around, I know that's not possible. So what do we do?

I go back to the advice of the first pediatrician my first child ever had: Just love them. And pray.

Your Fence is Broken

When we moved into our house four years ago, we hired a company to install an underground invisible fence in our yard. We wanted to keep our beloved GoldenDoodle, Dakota, safe from cars on the road and we wanted to keep our neighbors' yards safe from Doodle doody.

We put a special collar on Dakota and walked her slowly and gently around the yard, demonstrating where she could and couldn't venture. She's a smart dog and got the gist of the game in less than an hour.

Four years later, when she's wearing her special collar, she knows she can't leave the yard. Not even if a super exciting squirrel is provoking her from a forbidden tree. She'll stand there and bark, but she won't leave our yard.

But here's the thing, the fence is broken. It hasn't worked in about two years and I'm too cheap to get it fixed, because Dakota doesn't know it's broken.

When we put on her special collar, she still believes she will get hurt if she goes beyond the boundary.

I'm wondering if you have an invisible fence in your yard. Not your real yard, but the yard in your mind. Is there something someone once told you you couldn't do and now you blindly believe them?

Maybe that person told you "no" to keep you safe, or because it was best for them or because they were flat out mean. There are lots of reasons people set up fences for us.

I had an art teacher in third grade who returned my brilliant watercolor with a big red C at the top. Now, more than 30 years later, I still believe I'm terrible at anything artistic. I don't even try anymore. It's my invisible fence.

Friend, the fence is turned off. It's broken. If there is something you've always wanted to try, go for it. The space beyond the yard is wide open and it's waiting for you to frolick.

I think I'll pull out my colored pencils today and create something magnificent. How about you?

In Conclusion...

As I mentioned earlier in this book, I got a two-star review from a reader after I published my first book, *Kindness is Contagious: 100 Stories to Remind You God is Good and So Are Most People*. She was disappointed because she thought the stories should all be from the viewpoint of people who receive kindness, not the ones giving it.

I think maybe it felt a little braggy to her, people doing an act of kindness and then telling people about it.

I get it. I really do. I had many long conversations with God when I first started writing my newspaper column back in 2011.

I grew up hearing phrases like, "Don't let your left hand know what your right hand is doing" and "If you get credit for good acts on Earth, you won't get them in Heaven."

You know what God said to me about that? Hogwash.

Okay, maybe those weren't His exact words, but the meaning was there.

God put a great peace in my heart by teaching me it's the motivation behind the act of kindness that matters. If we give away millions of dollars specifically hoping to become a YouTube sensation, well then, maybe YouTube is our ultimate reward.

But if we do something kind that opens up a beautiful interaction and increases love in the world, then that's worth sharing.

In fact, it's important to share those stories because it reminds people it's not just those with excess time, money and energy who can be radically kind. It can be all of us. We don't need an abundance of anything to love on the people who cross our paths. We just need to be brave.

Here's another great reason to shout about kindness from the mountaintops. According to my friends at the Random Acts of Kindness Foundation, kindness works as a trifecta. The giver, the receiver and the witness all benefit from a release of feel-good chemicals during an act of kindness. That's why it's so important to fill our social media feeds with inspiring stories and uplifting videos. Kindness can balance out some of the other things we might feel when we scroll through other people's lives, so we set down the phone feeling encouraged instead of deflated.

Back to that two-star review. I texted my best friend, Andrea, when I read it. I would have called, but I was crying. (Yes, I occasionally overreact in life.) Andrea went to Amazon and took a screen shot of my favorite book's review section. It was filled with two star reviews. You know what that book was? The Bible. Even the best-selling book of all time doesn't please everyone all the time.

The great kindness to me in this story is that Andrea doesn't read the Bible. She's not a Jesus follower, but she knows that I am. So she gave me what she knew I needed in that moment. Not sympathy or words of encouragement, but proof that I was on the right path regardless of what others may say.

I have been called to share stories of kindness.

And so have you.

If you've been the giver, receiver or witness of a fun act of kindness, I'd love for you to send me your story at info@nicolejphillips.com or through my website at www.braveandkind.net.

YOU are brave and kind. May you always know the power of kindness in your life.

Thank you

I would like to thank the following people for bringing this book to life:

*Bill Marcil, Jr., publisher of *The Forum of Fargo-Moorhead* who continues to encourage the people around him to dream big.

*My editors at *The Forum* who work hard each week to make me look good and save me a spot in the Lifestyle section.

*My Kindness Team: Teresa South, Amanda Koenecke and Sarah Tachon, whose initials are in the artwork on the front cover of this book. I dreamed you would come into my life one day, but I never imagined it would be this much fun.

*Stacey Piechowski, who thankfully loves to read and take notes more than anyone else I know. If you ever need an editor, call Stacey!

*Saul, to everyone else you are Coach, but to me you are the World's Best Cheerleader. Thank you for loving me well.

*Jordan (14), Charlie (12) & Ben (8), you hold me accountable to kindness and remind me daily why sharing these stories is so important. I love you kiddos.

*Caleb and Marcus, I treasure you. I can't wait to see how you change the world with your compassionate hearts.

*To everyone who has been brave enough to send me your stories of kindness, thank you. It is an honor to share your words.

About the Author

Nicole J Phillips is a champion for using kindness to overcome all of life's difficulties, including her own battle with breast cancer. She spreads the message of the healing power of kindness as host of her weekly show, The Kindness Podcast, and through her column, *Kindness is Contagious*, which runs each Friday in newspapers in North Dakota and Minnesota. She is also the author of the book, *Kindness is Contagious: 100 Stories to Remind You God is Good and So Are Most People.*

Nicole has her Broadcast Journalism degree from the University of Wisconsin and has worked as a television anchor and reporter in Milwaukee, Wisconsin, Madison, Wisconsin and Fargo, North Dakota. As Miss Wisconsin 1997, she spent the year touring the state talking to kids and adults about overcoming crisis. Now she loves traveling the nation, sharing her message of bravery and kindness as a tool for increasing wellness.

Nicole lives in Athens, Ohio, has three children and is married to Ohio University Men's Basketball Coach, Saul Phillips.

Connect with Nicole at www.nicolejphillips.com.

CPSIA information can be obtained
at www.ICGtesting.com
Printed in the USA
LVHW03s1553150818
587067LV00016B/1698/P